" Memento mori "

Still Life with Death
Still Life with Prey & Vanitas

Still Life with Prey and Vanitas is an artistic genre that explores the common theme of the transience of life and death.

Still Life with Prey typically refers to paintings depicting still lifes, including carcasses of animals or birds obtained through hunting. This genre shares its theme with Vanitas works, which were popular in the 17th century Netherlands. Vanitas, centered around decaying flowers, rotten fruits, clocks, skulls, and other symbols, symbolizes the impermanence of life and inevitability of death. It conveys a message that all earthly pleasures and achievements lose their significance in the face of death. In the 17th century Netherlands and Flanders (part of present-day Belgium), such themes became central to artistic exploration. This era, known as the Dutch Golden Age, witnessed significant prosperity in commerce, maritime trade, arts, and sciences. Contemporary artists demonstrated exceptional talent in capturing the beauty and simple joys of everyday life through still life paintings. They depicted animals obtained through hunting with intricate and realistic detail, interpreting the transience of life, the beauty of nature, and the societal importance of hunting. The genre of Still Life with Prey gained popularity across Europe, but the delicate techniques and profound symbolic interpretations developed particularly in the Netherlands and Flanders significantly contributed to its evolution. Many artists, such as Frans Snyders and Willem Van Aelst, left notable works in this genre.

Artists & Paintings

Abraham Hendrickz. van Beyeren
1637 - 1690

Abraham Hendricksz. Van Beyeren was a Dutch painter active in the 17th century, renowned for his still life paintings that lavishly depict everyday objects. He received art education in The Hague and joined the Guild of Saint Luke in Delft. Through ripe fruits, shimmering shells, and elaborate table settings, he created works that convey abundance. His paintings praise the material richness of nature and sensual pleasures alongside Vanitas elements, celebrating the beauty and richness of life. Notably, through still lifes featuring dead fish as motifs, he reflected on the transient nature of material wealth.

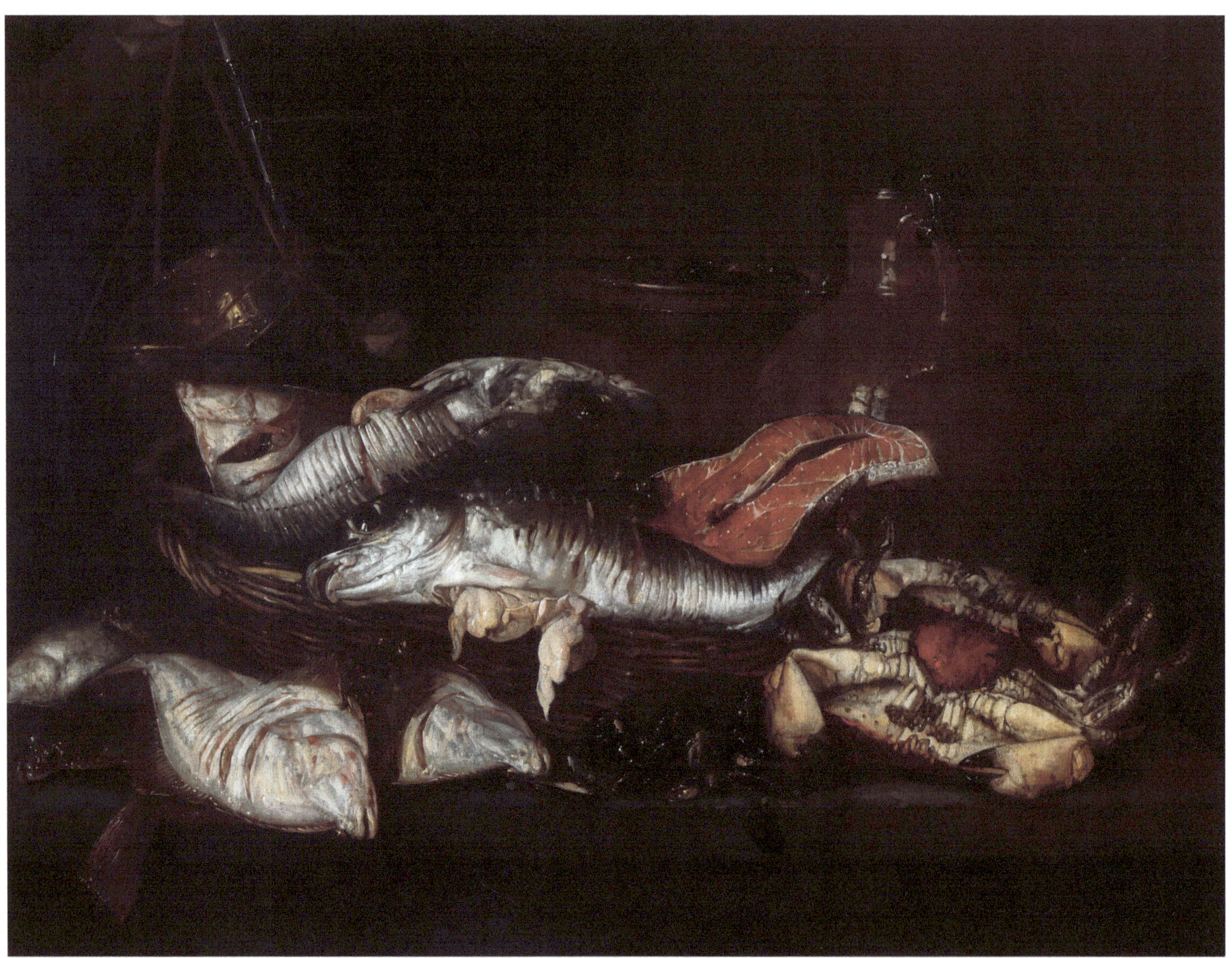

71.4 x 92.4 cm

Philadelphia Museum of Art

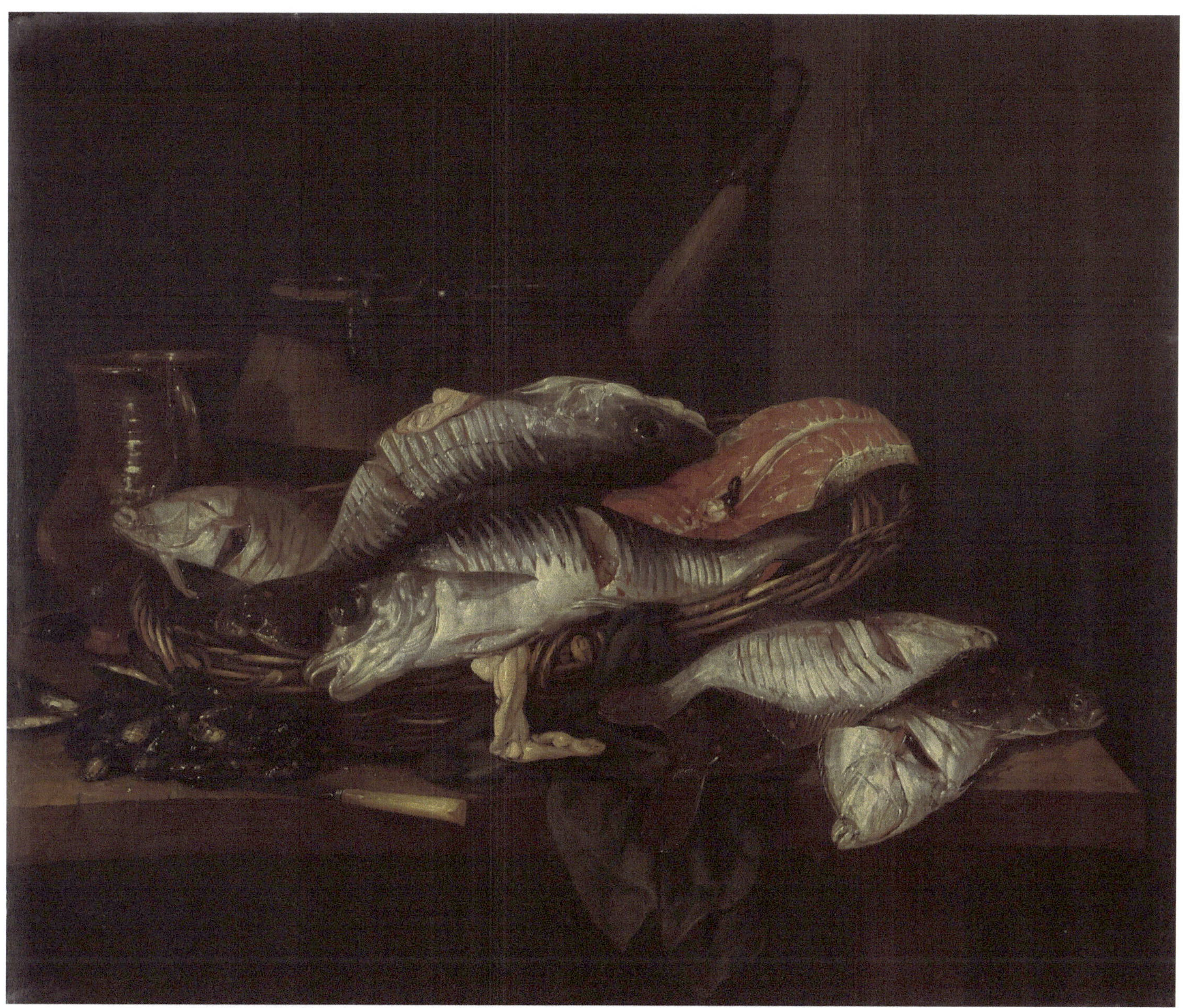

74 x 87 cm

Rijksmuseum Amsterdam

Abraham Hendrickz. van Beyeren

Still life with Fish, c.1650-90

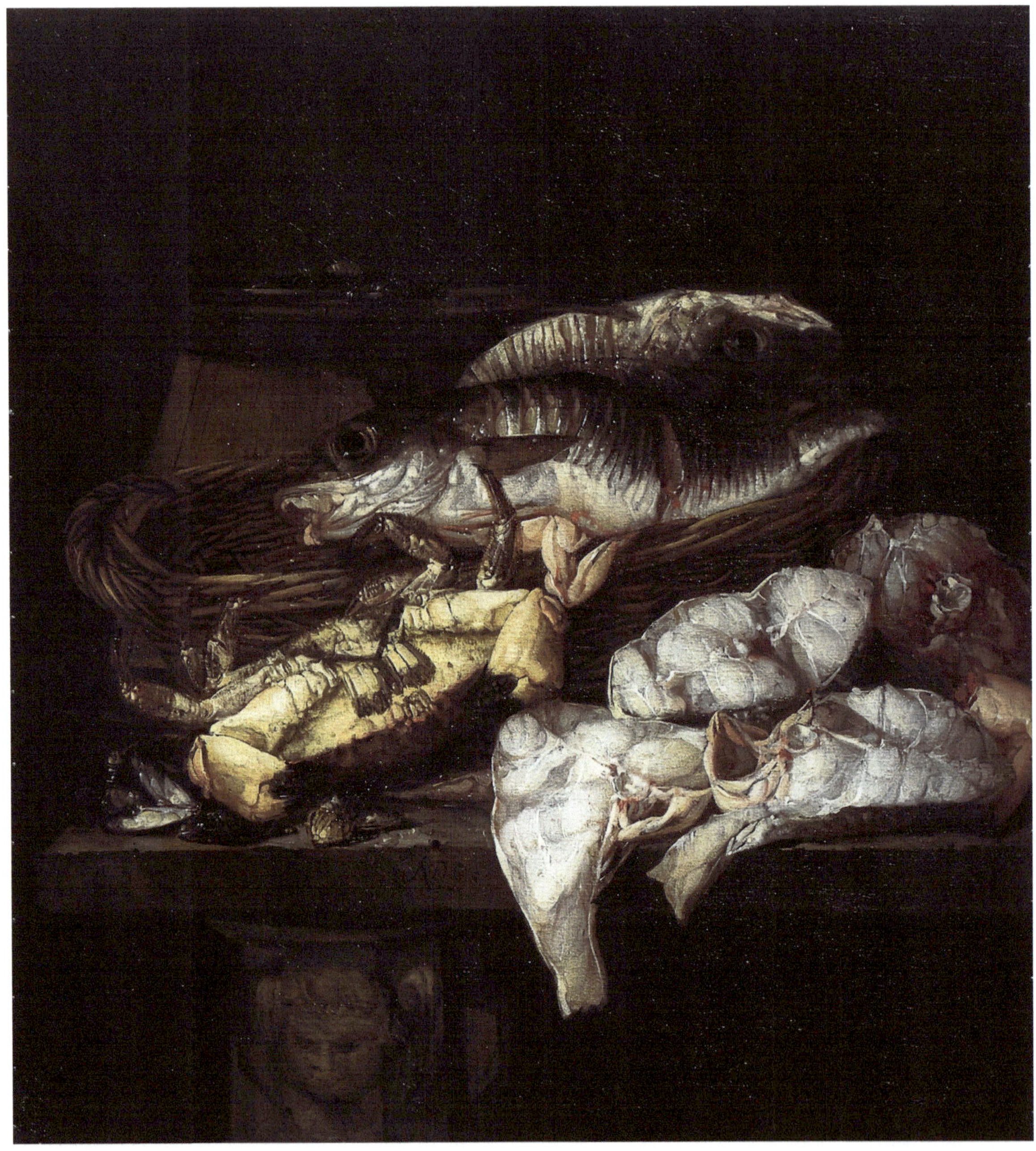

75.8 x 68 cm

The Royal Picture Gallery Mauritshuis

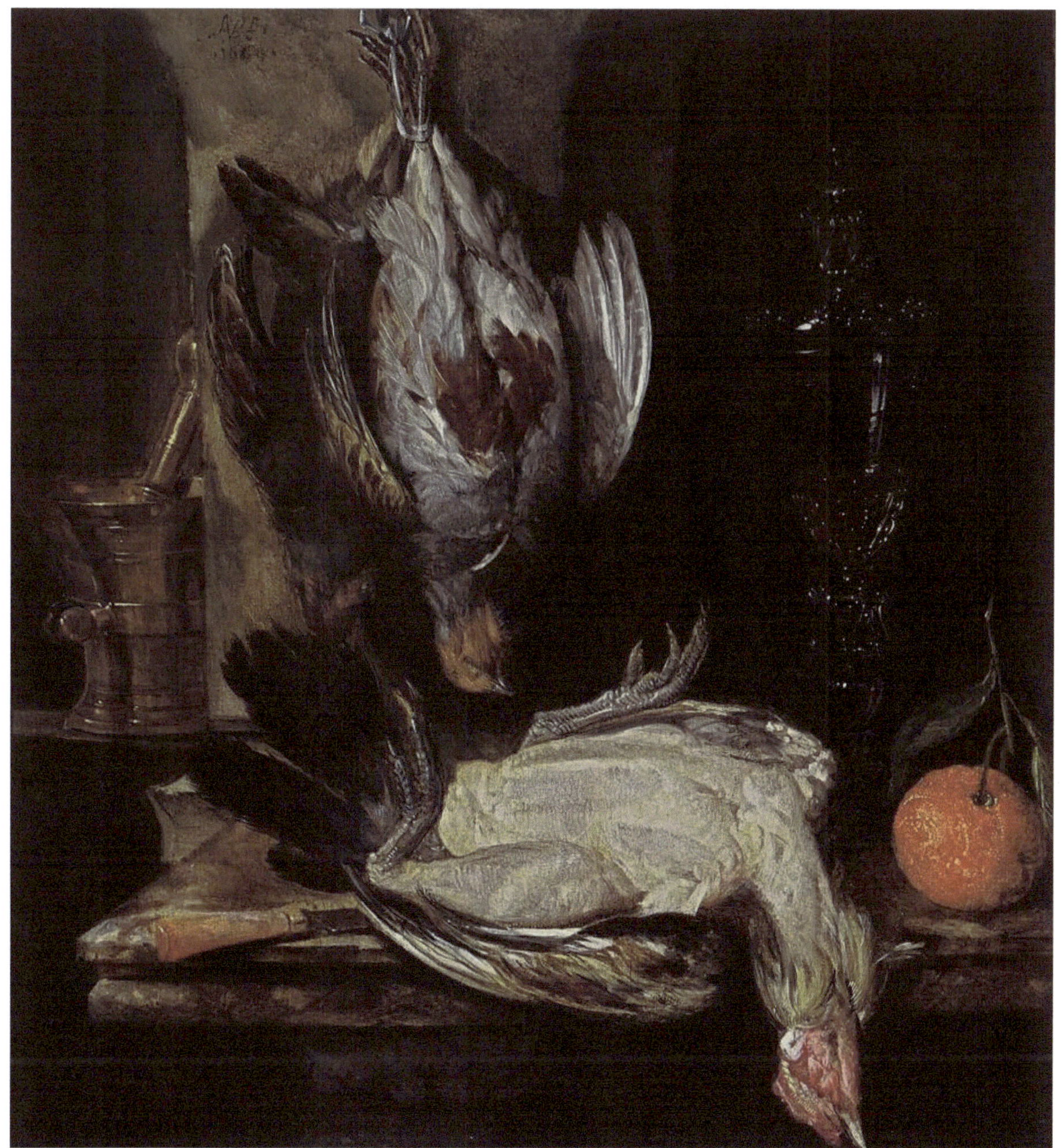

64 x 59 cm

Still life with Fruit and bat bird, 1651

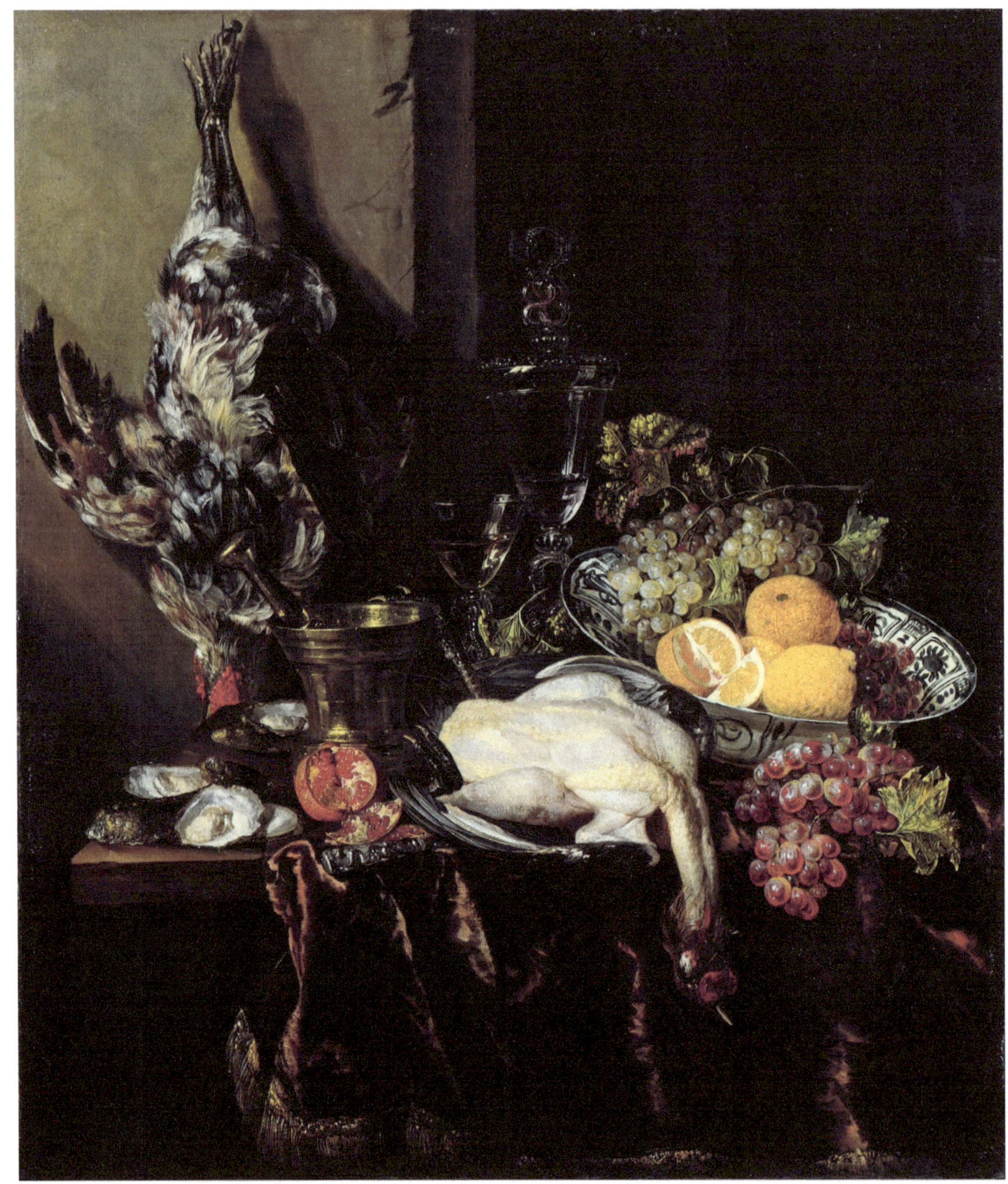

104 x 88.8 cm

The Kunstpalast Museum in Düsseldorf

Alexander Adriaenssen
1596 - 1661

Alexander Adriaensen is a renowned Flemish Baroque painter known for his contributions to the still life genre of the Dutch Golden Age. Specializing in the Vanitas genre that emerged in 16th-17th century Europe, he demonstrated exceptional skill in portraying the perishable nature of objects by rendering various textures and surfaces vividly. Adriaensen intricately arranged symbolic elements in his works, creating visually rich compositions. In addition to typical Vanitas motifs, he integrated religious symbols and references into his paintings, occasionally incorporating scenes from the Bible, religious texts, or devout objects to imbue the artwork with a spiritual dimension. Through these religious undertones, the earthly possessions and pursuits depicted ultimately underscore the futility in the face of death and eternity. Today, his works are held in prestigious collections worldwide, such as the Royal Museum of Fine Arts in Antwerp and the Royal Museums of Fine Arts of Belgium in Brussels, and they continue to be studied for their complex symbolism, exceptional execution, and profound thematic exploration of the human condition facing mortality.

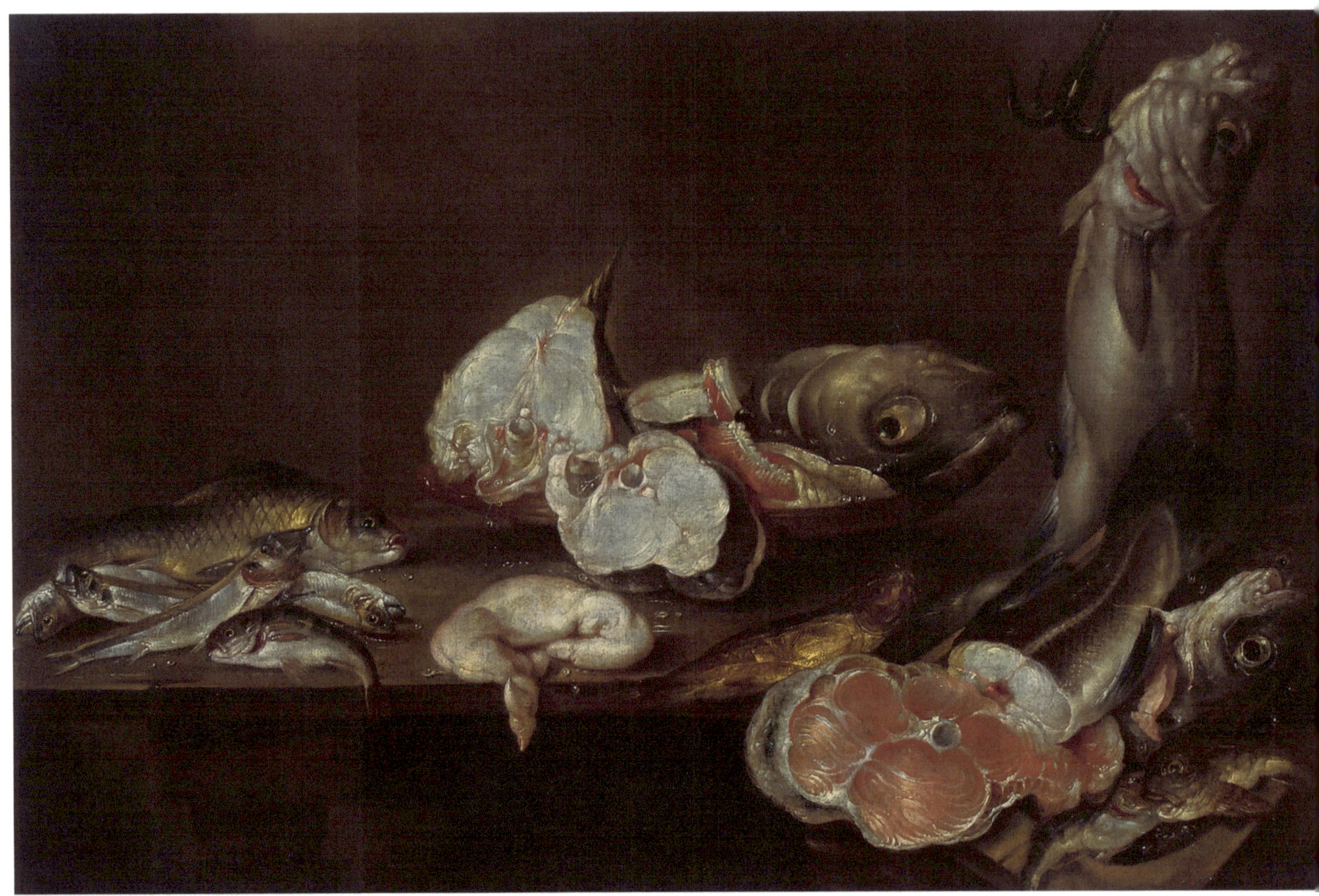

59.5 x 85 cm

State Hermitage Museum

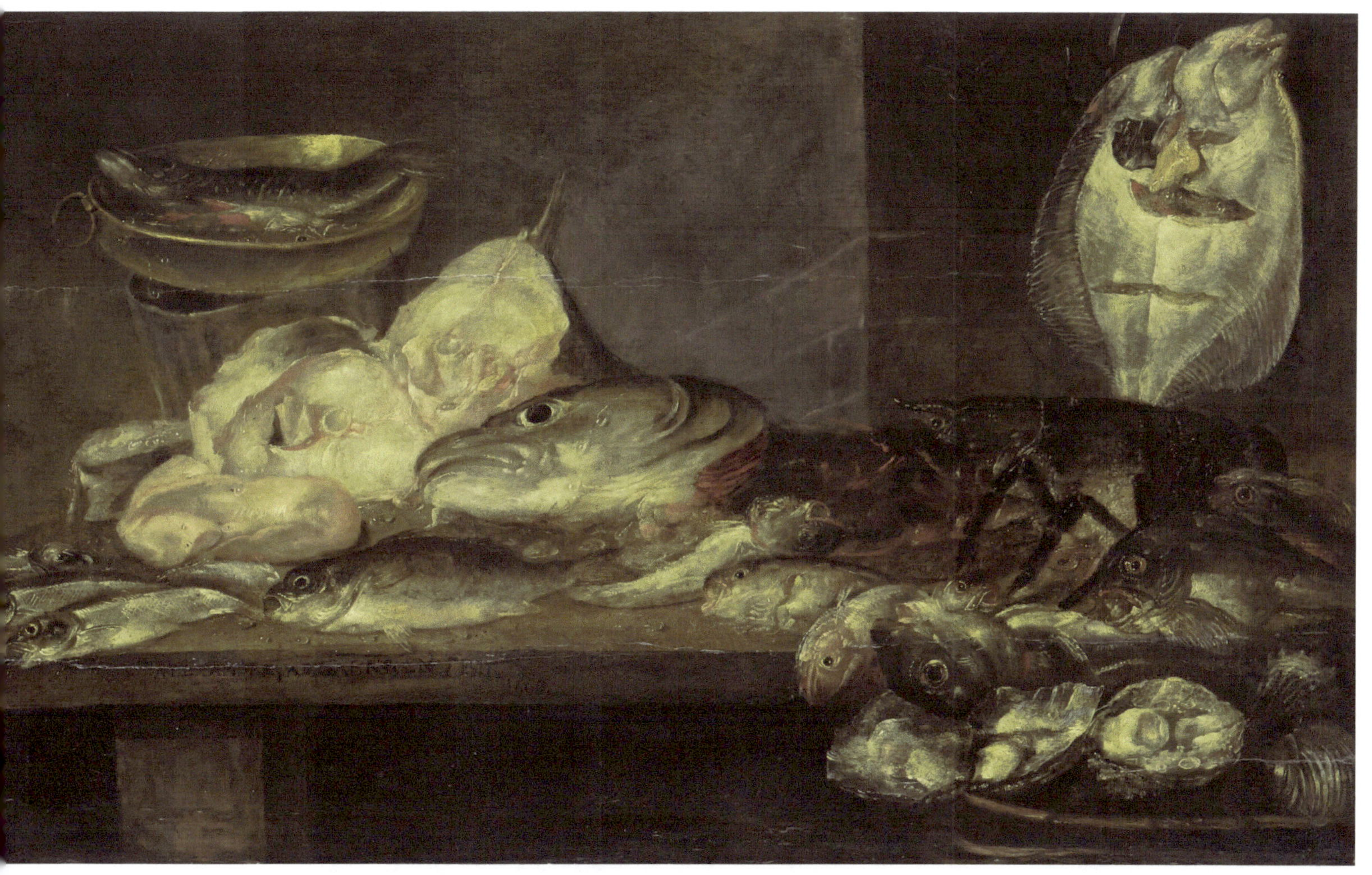

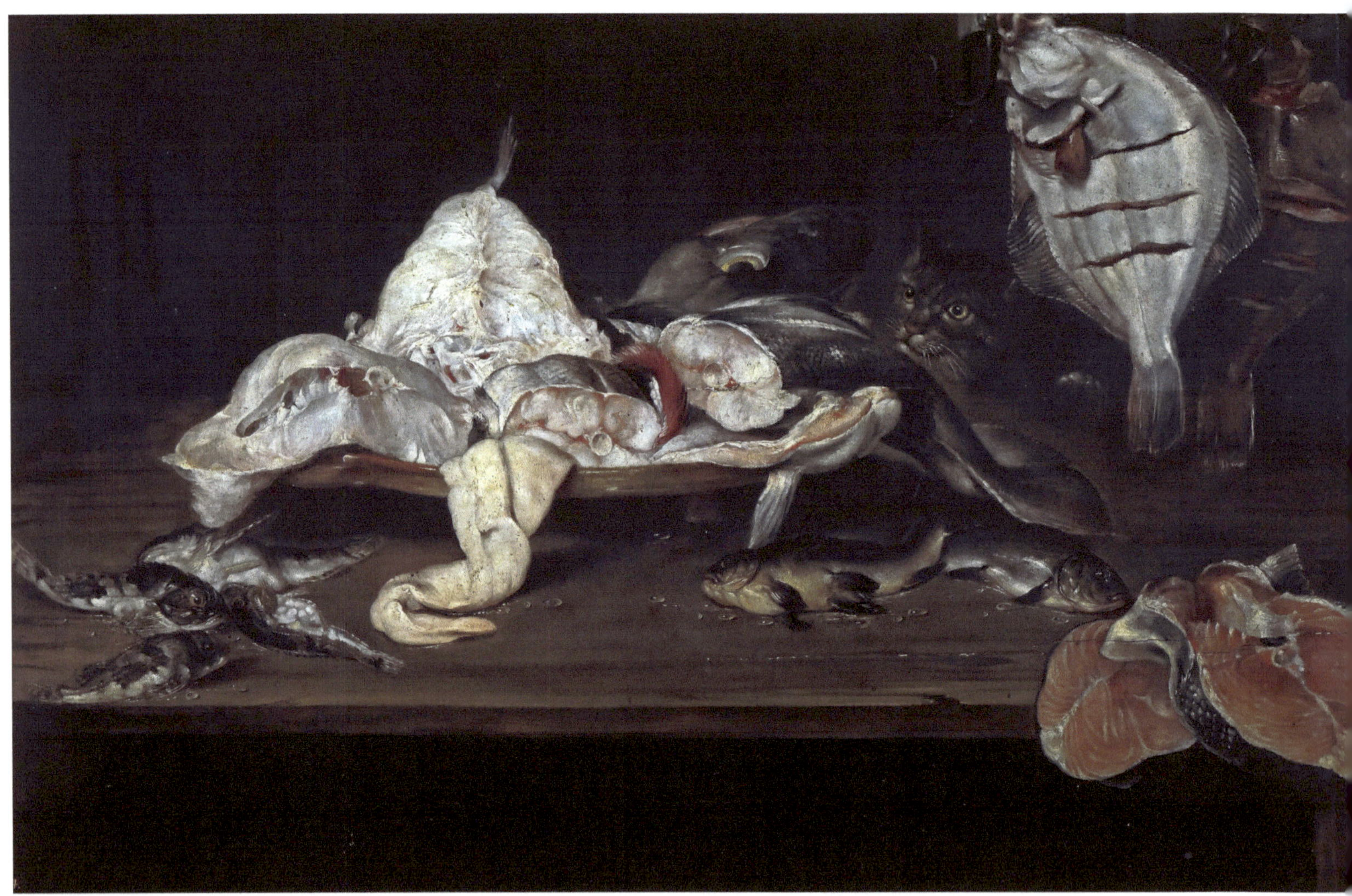

59 x 91 cm

Prado Museum in Madrid

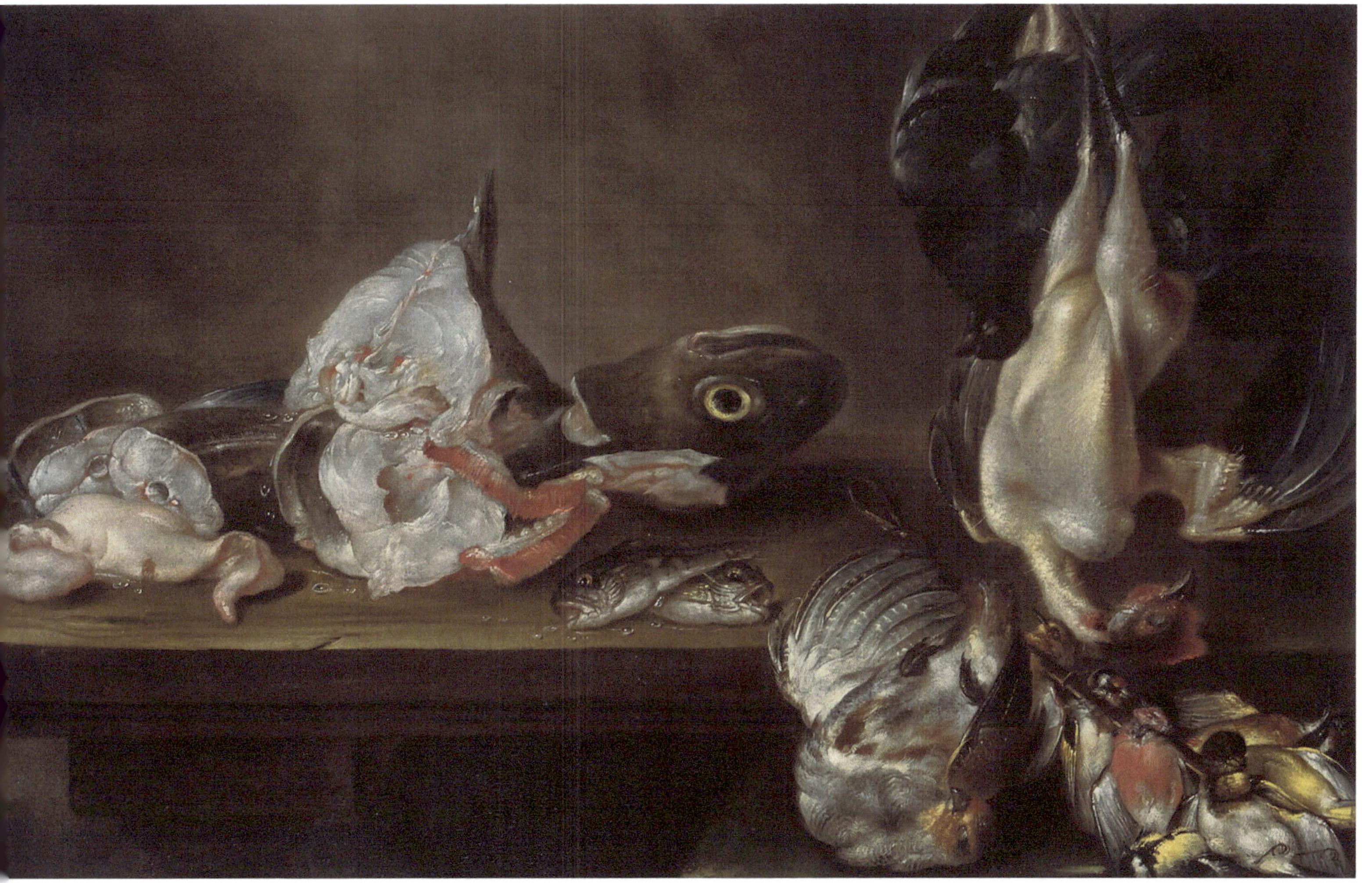

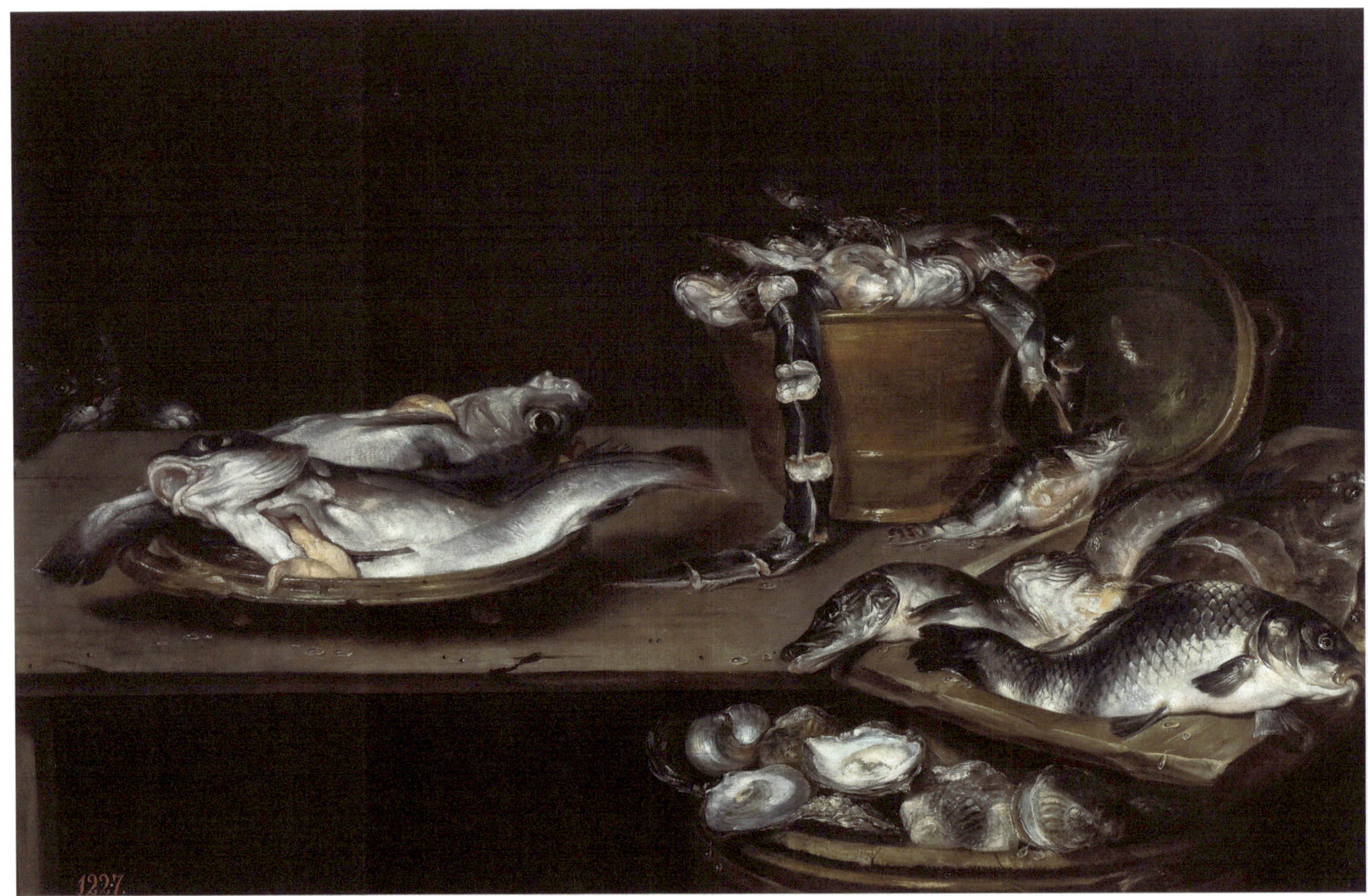

60 x 91 cm

Still life with a bird

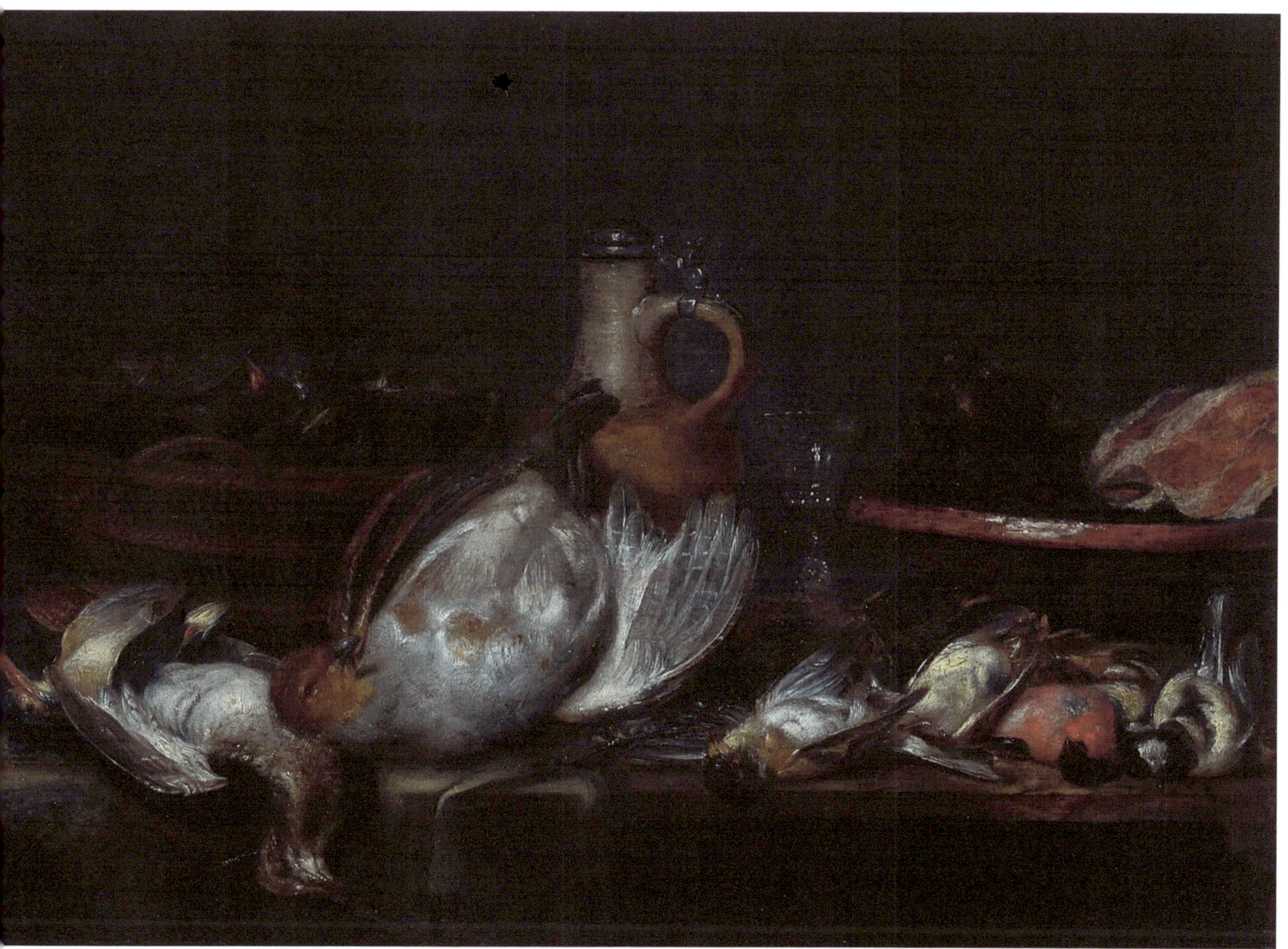

50 x 66 cm

Warsaw Royal Castle Museum

Still life with fish and game, 1632

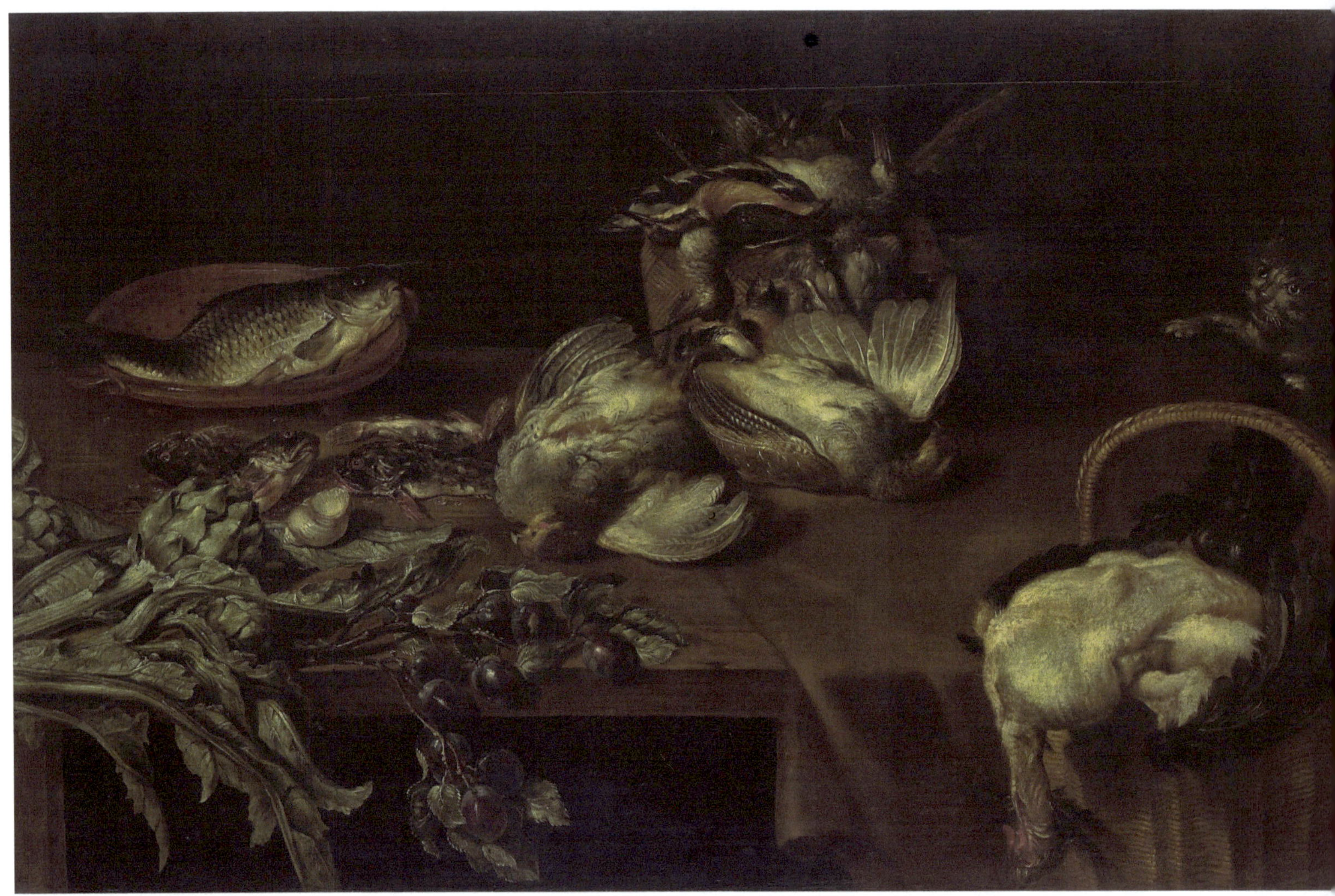

74 x 114 cm

Rijksmuseum Amsterdam

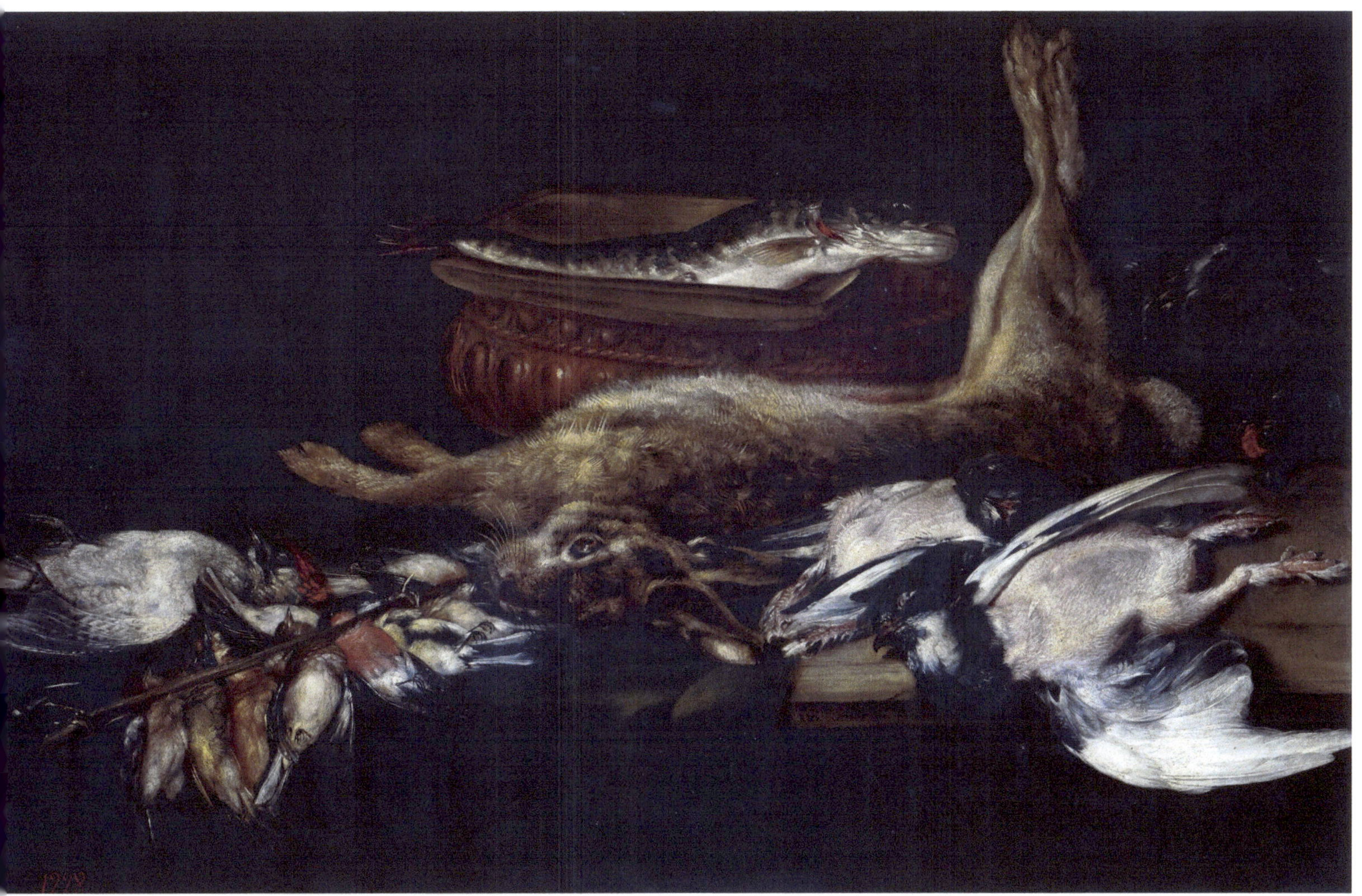

Clara Peeters
c.1588/94 - 1621

Clara Peeters was born in 1588 (or estimated to be 1594) in Antwerp, Belgium, a hub of 17th-century art. Despite restrictions on women's participation in the arts and guild membership, she was one of the few women artists to actively pursue a professional career. Peeters excelled in the still life genre, particularly in balanced compositions of table settings and hunting scenes. She meticulously depicted not only fruits, seafood, bread, and elegant tableware but also the carcasses of animals obtained through hunting. Beyond everyday objects, Clara Peeters explored profound themes such as the relationship between humans and nature and the cycle of life through her hunting still lifes. Her works, which demonstrate profound reflections on life, death, and the passage of time, were widely acclaimed during her lifetime.

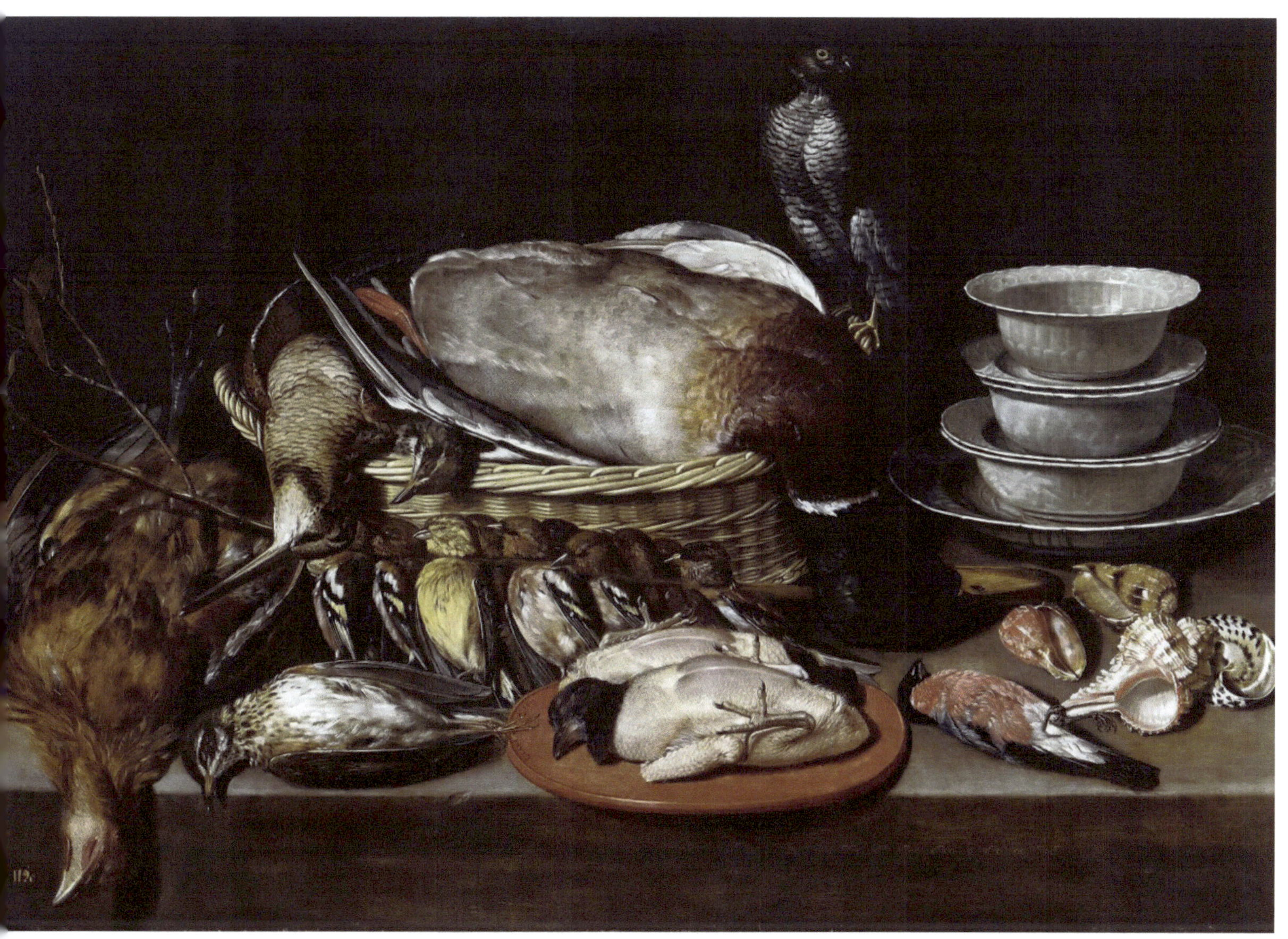

52 x 71 cm

Frans Snyders
1579 - 1657

   Born in Antwerp, Belgium in 1579, Frans Snyders is renowned as a Flemish Baroque painter, famous for his still life and flower-themed works. With a profound interest in the relationship between animals and humans, Snyders, influenced by the grandeur and splendor of Baroque art, produced numerous vibrant works centered around animals. He pioneered the combination of still life and animal subjects, expressing the intimate connection between humans and nature through works centered around hunting. While emphasizing the pursuit of leisure by the nobility, he also explored the primal relationship between humans and the animal kingdom.

Furthermore, by depicting the transience of life and the futility of earthly pleasures in his still lifes and animal paintings, he constructed a world of art that resonated with the Vanitas theme. Lavishly set tables, exotic fruits, and luxurious vessels hinted at the ephemeral nature of worldly wealth and the inevitability of decay. Hunted game and various states of animals were used as elements to evoke thoughts of mortality. Collaborating with contemporary artists such as Peter Paul Rubens, Snyders left a profound impact on the art world with his unique style and passed away in 1657.

Fish Shop, 1620s

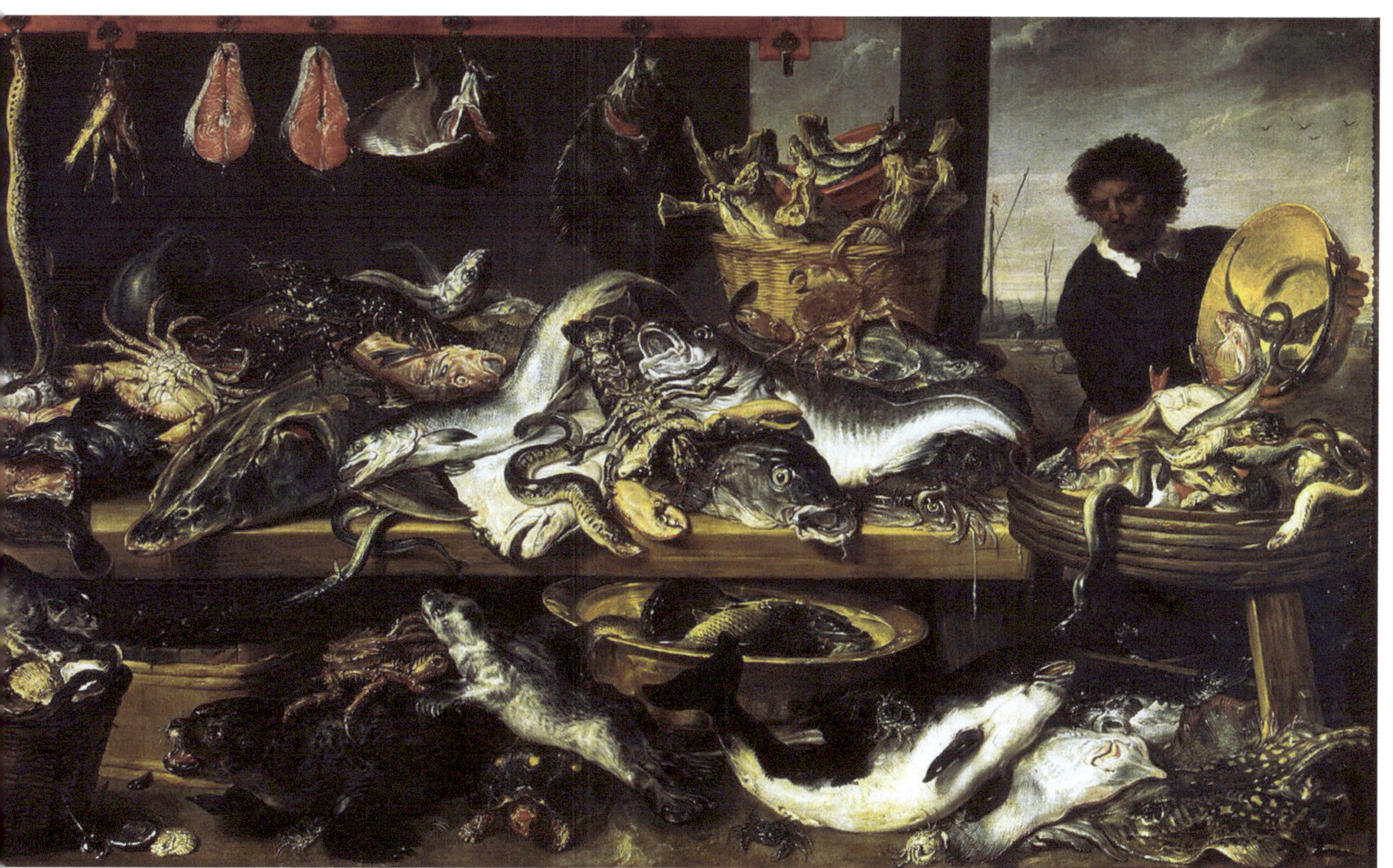

209.5 x 341 cm

The State Hermitage Museum in Saint Petersburg

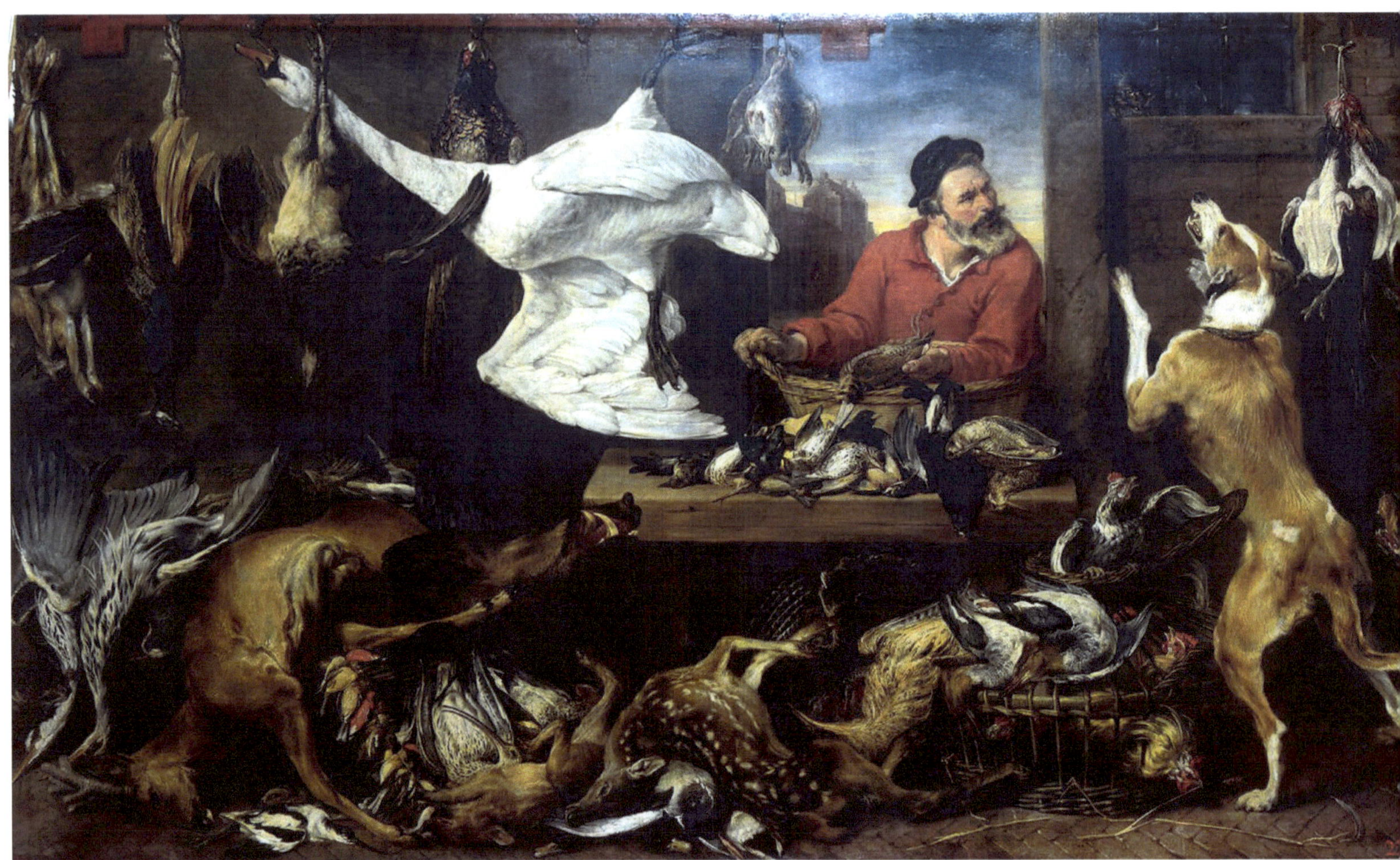

207 x 341 cm

The State Hermitage Museum in Saint Petersburg

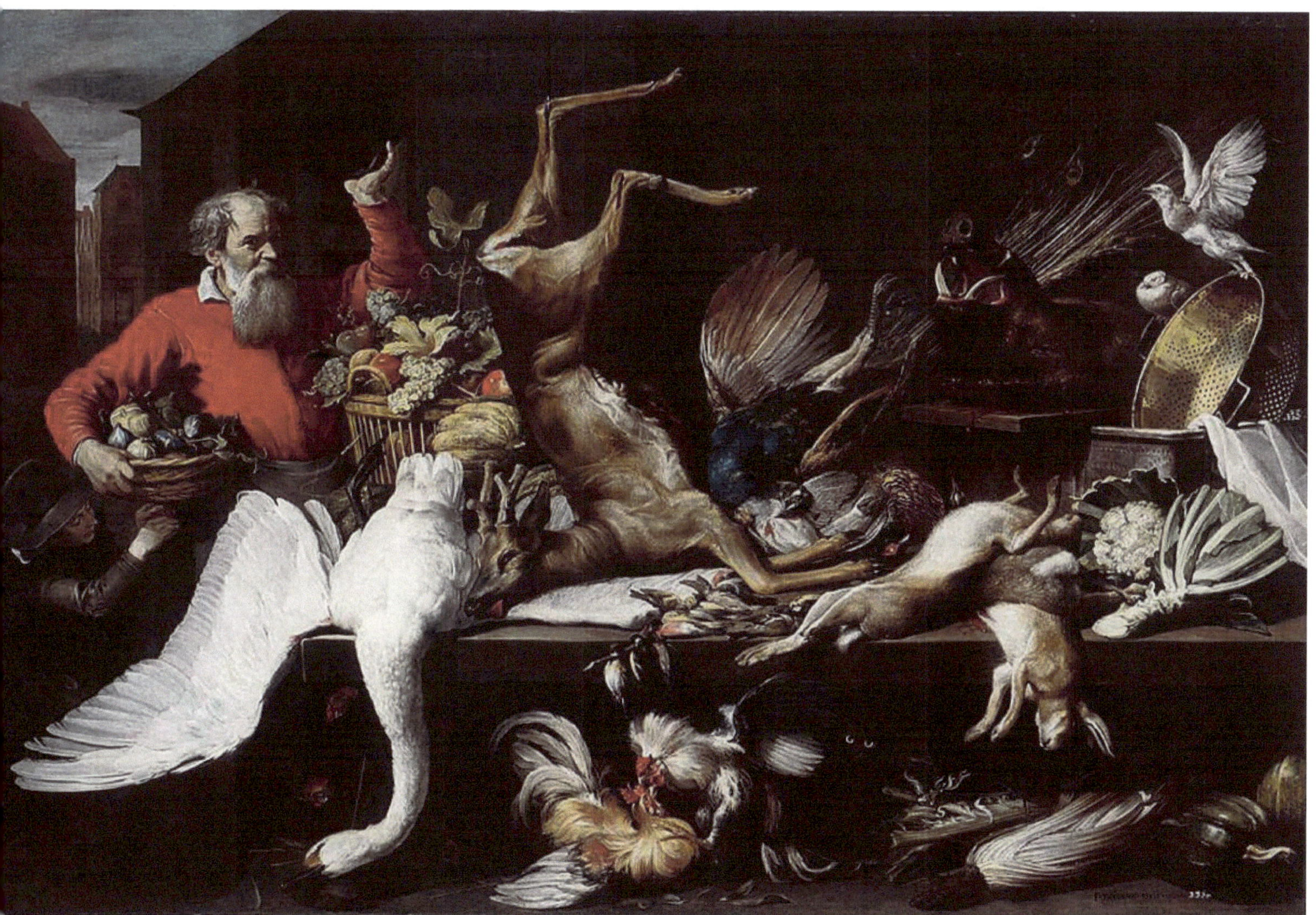

212 x 308 cm

The Art Institute of Chicago

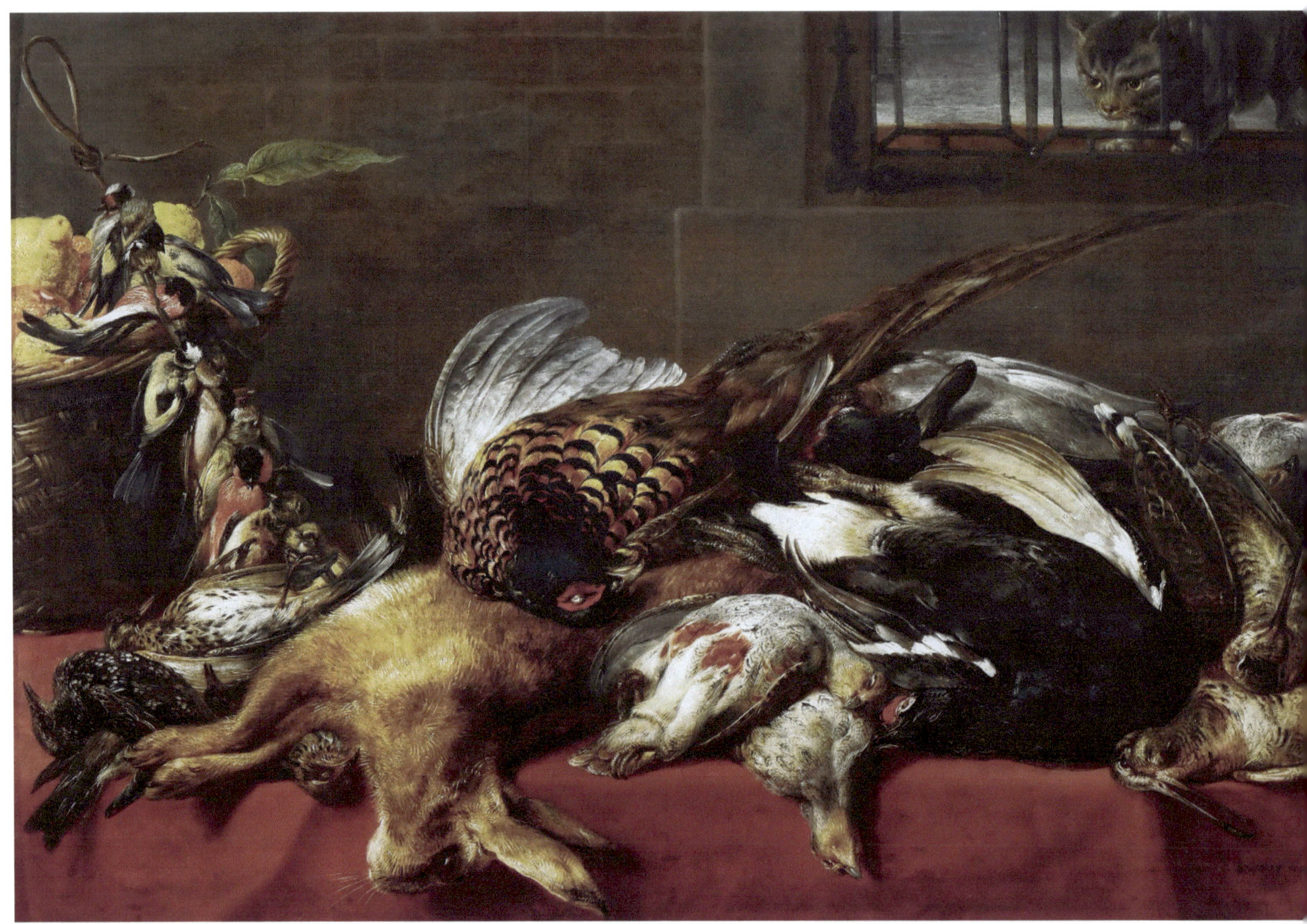

75 x 107 cm

Vienna Museum of Art History

Still life with roe and lobster

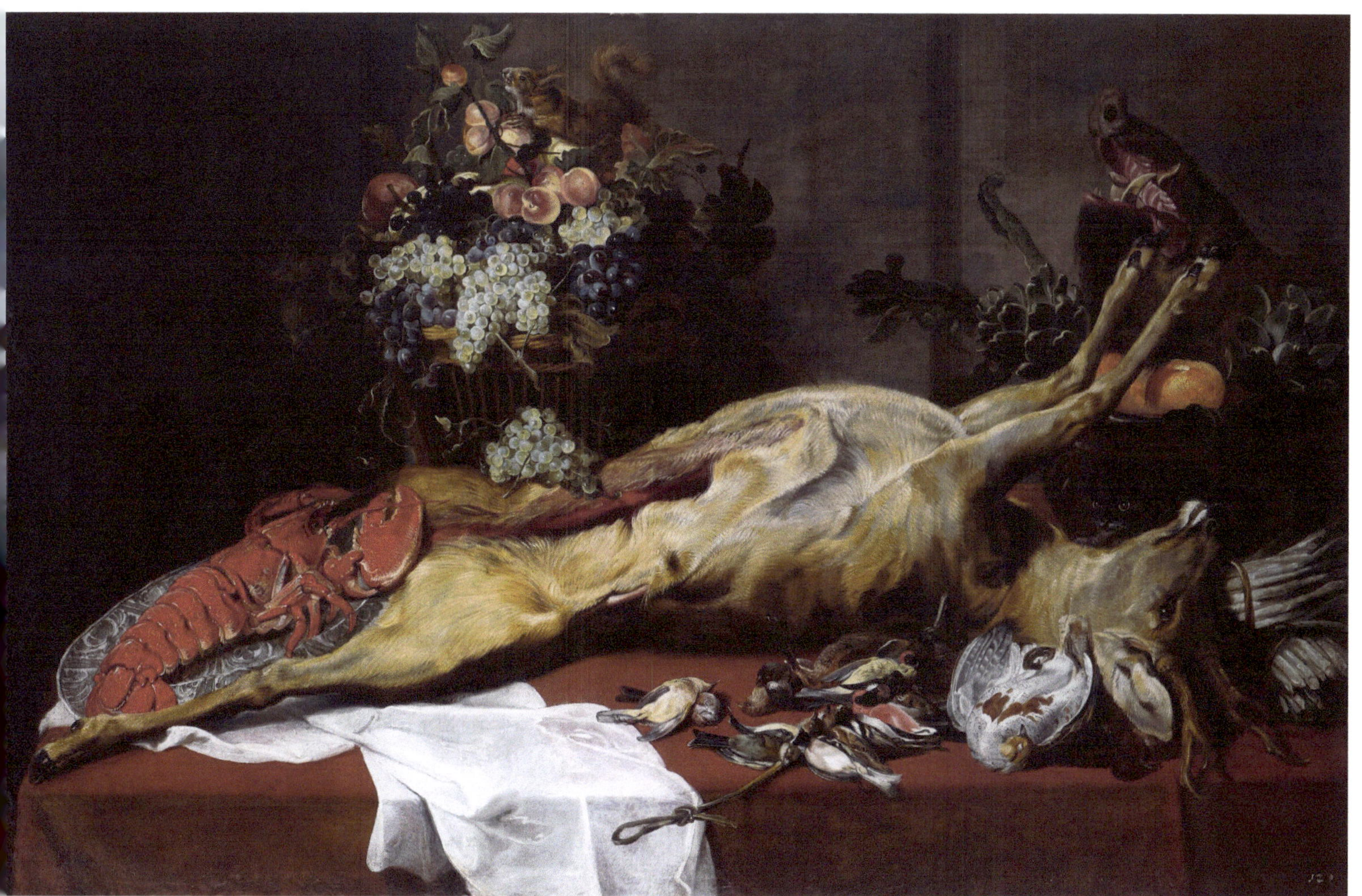

117 x 179 cm

The British Museum in London

Still life with a maid and a boy

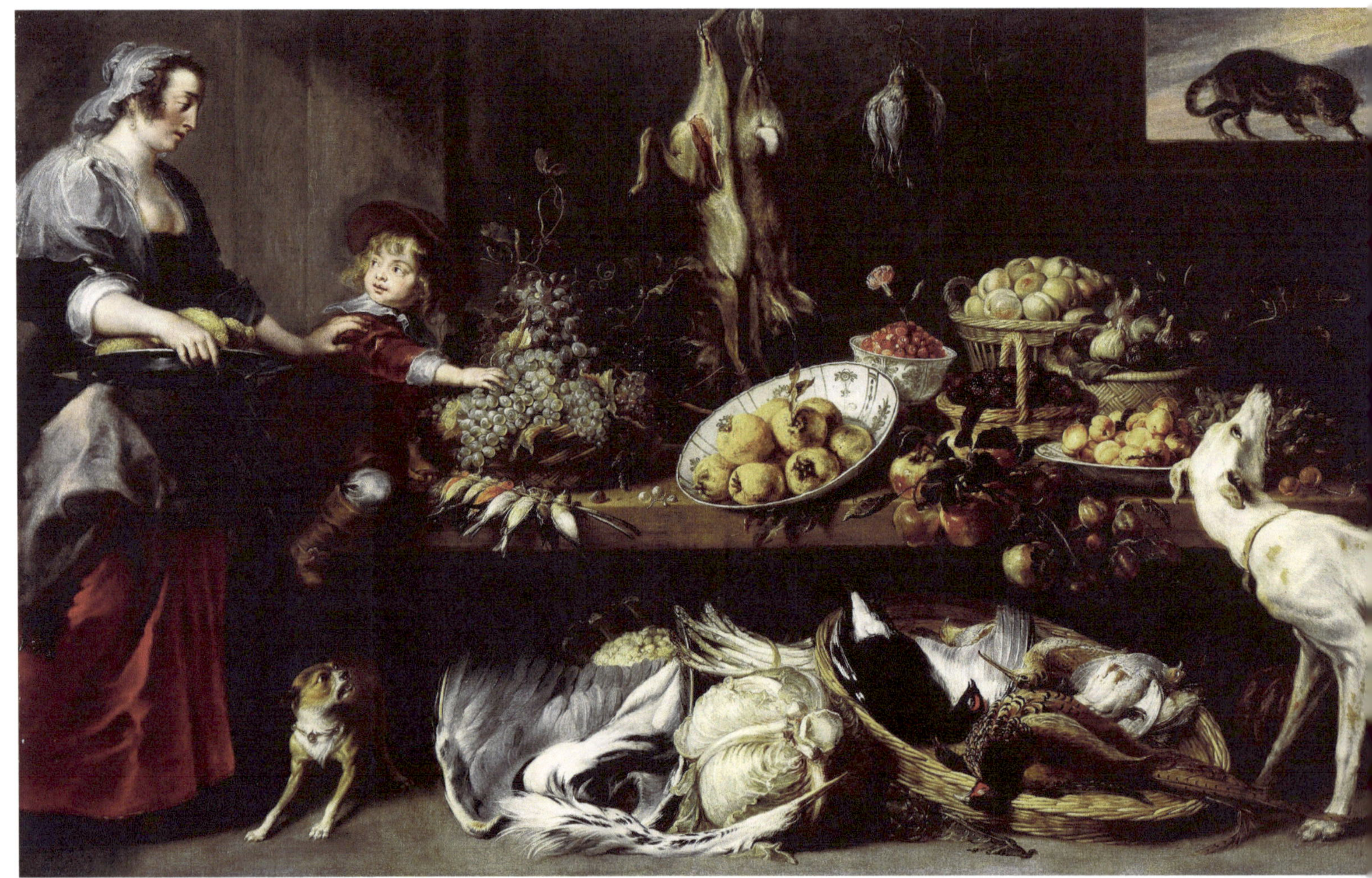

152 x 240 cm

The J. Paul Getty Museum in Los Angeles

Still life with a monkey

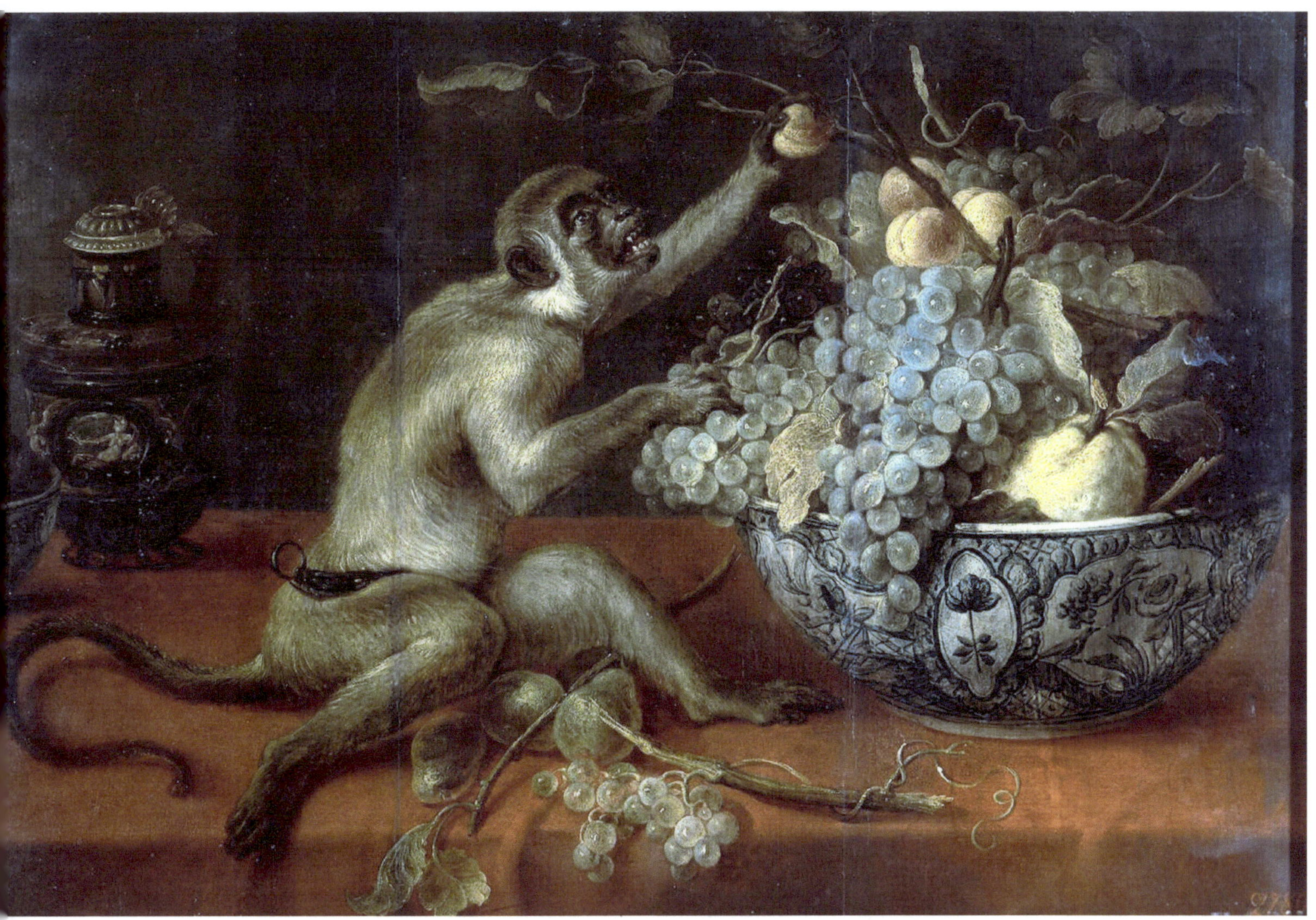

64 x 78 cm

The State Hermitage Museum in Saint Petersburg

Still life with a swan, 1640s

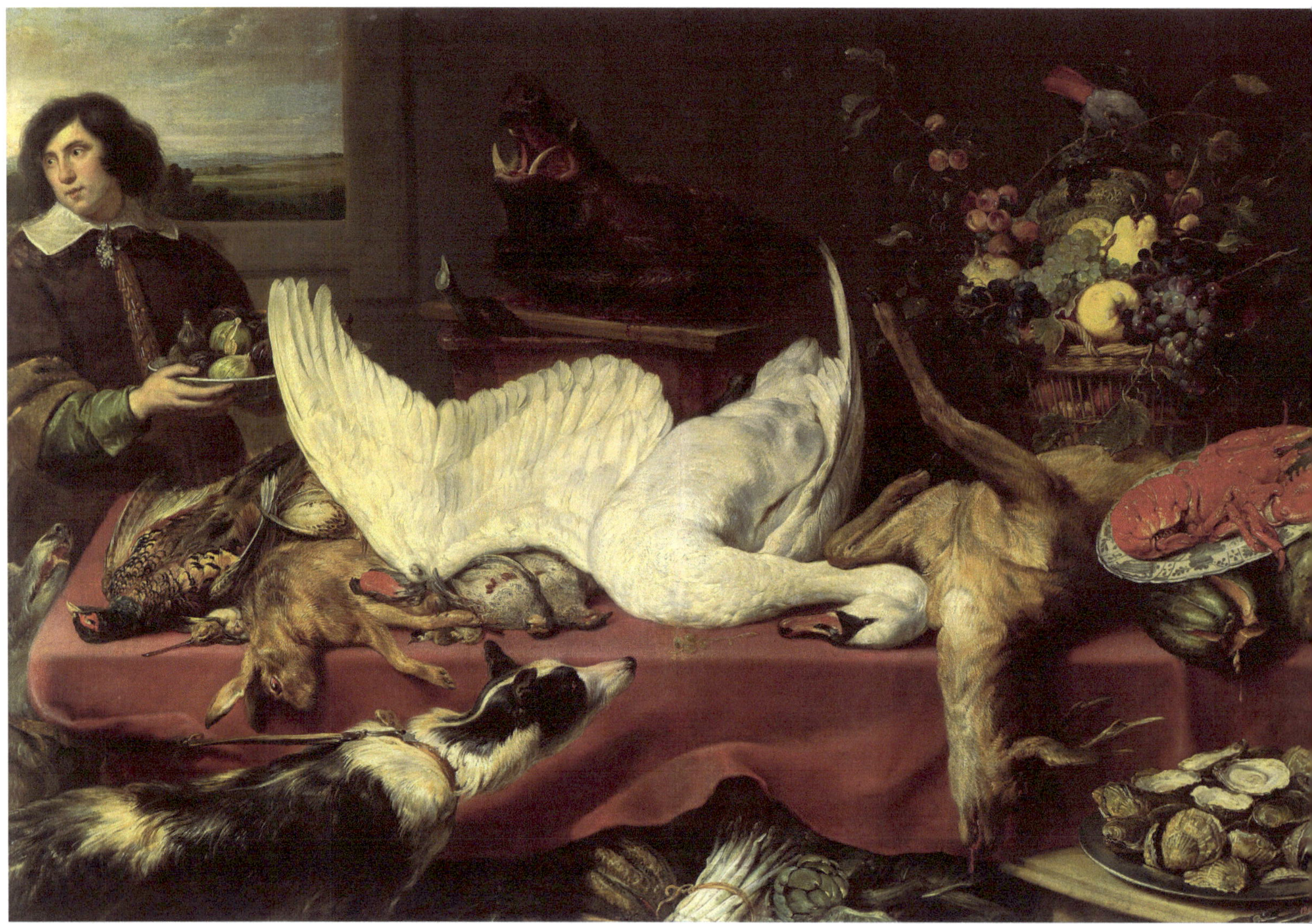

162.5 x 235 cm

The Pushkin State Museum of Fine Arts in Moscow

Still life with deer and wild boar head, lobster and fruit, c.1657

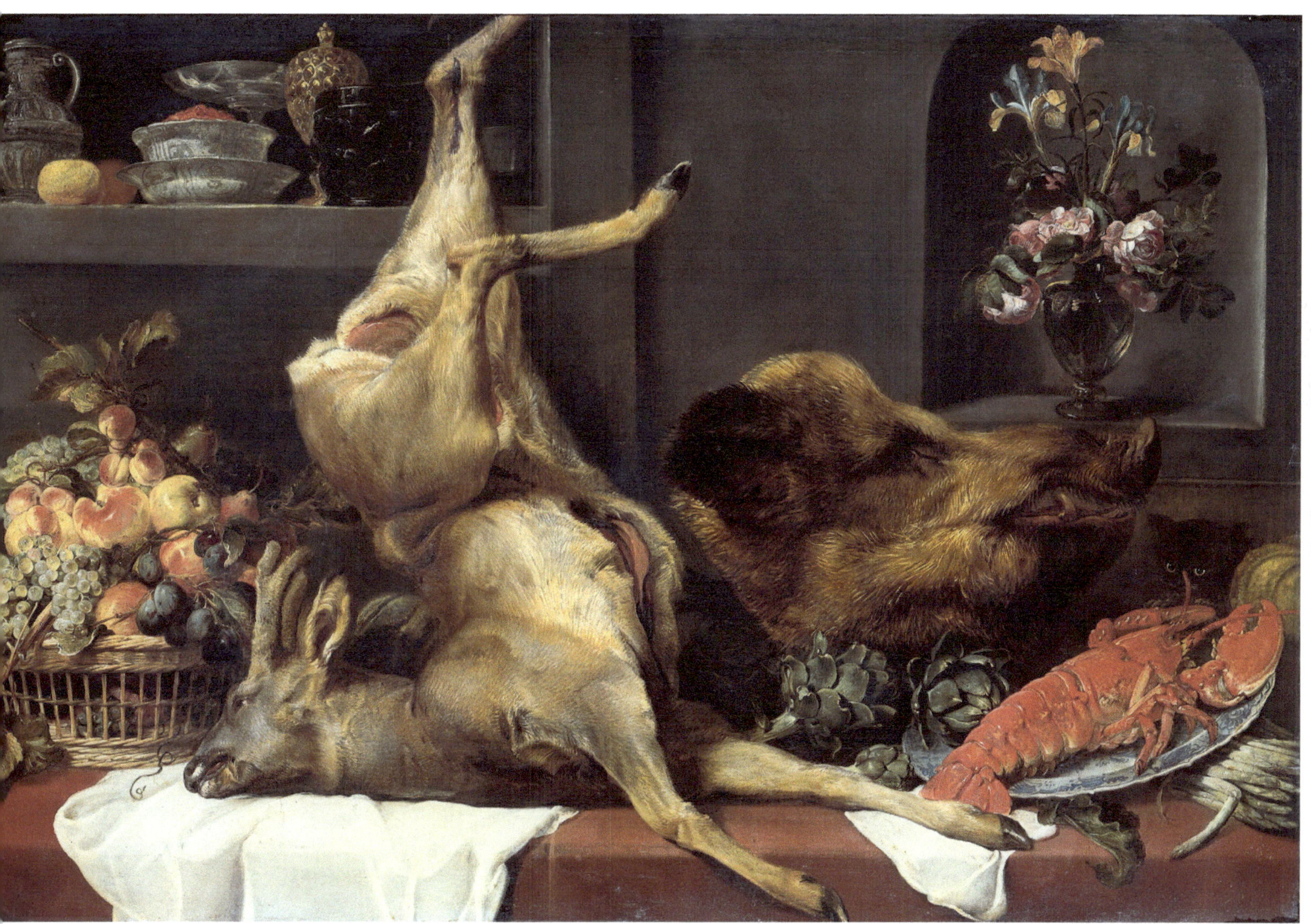

120.5 x 176.5 cm

Rijksmuseum Amsterdam

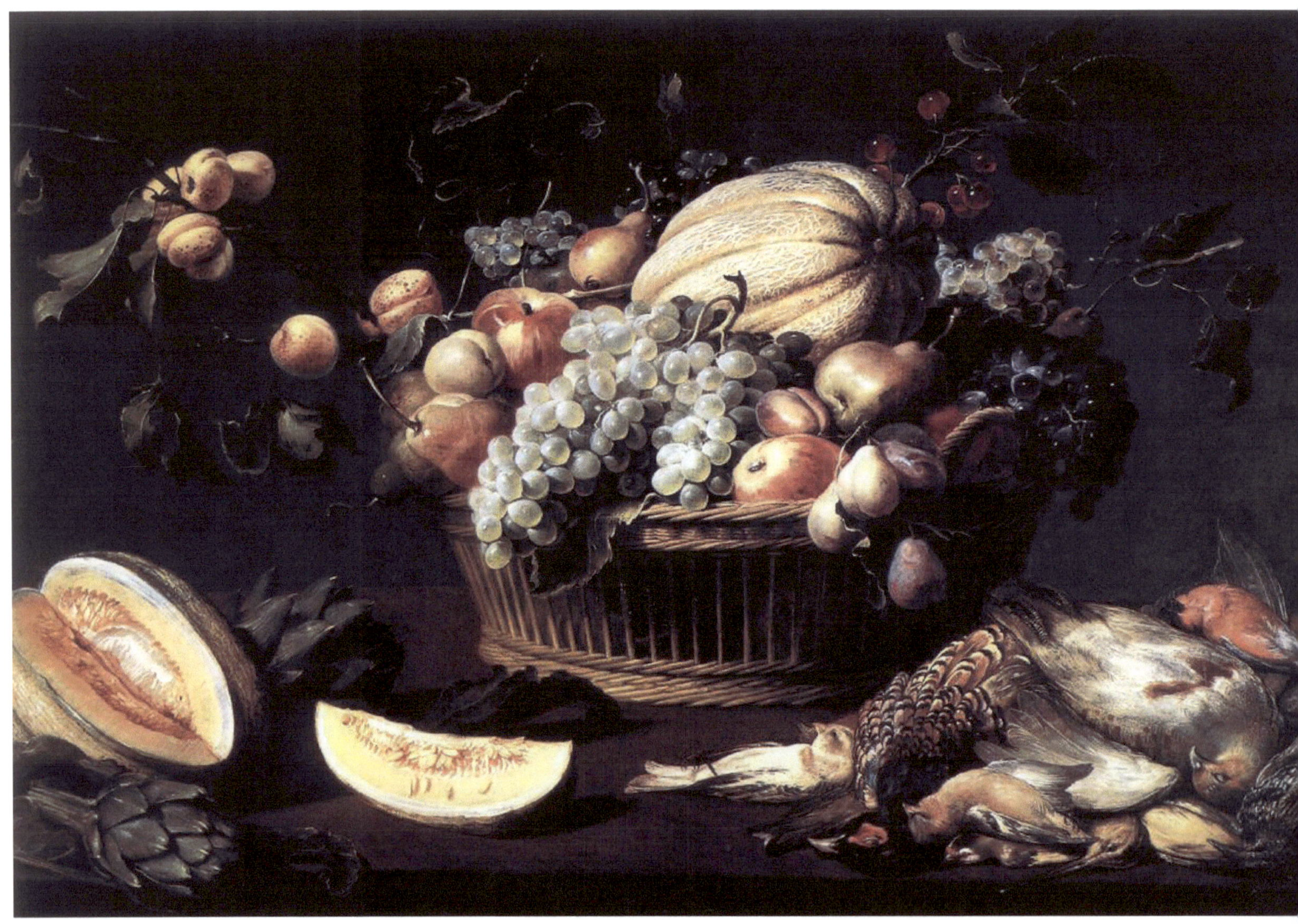

74 x 105 cm

The Rockox House in Antwerp

Still life with Game

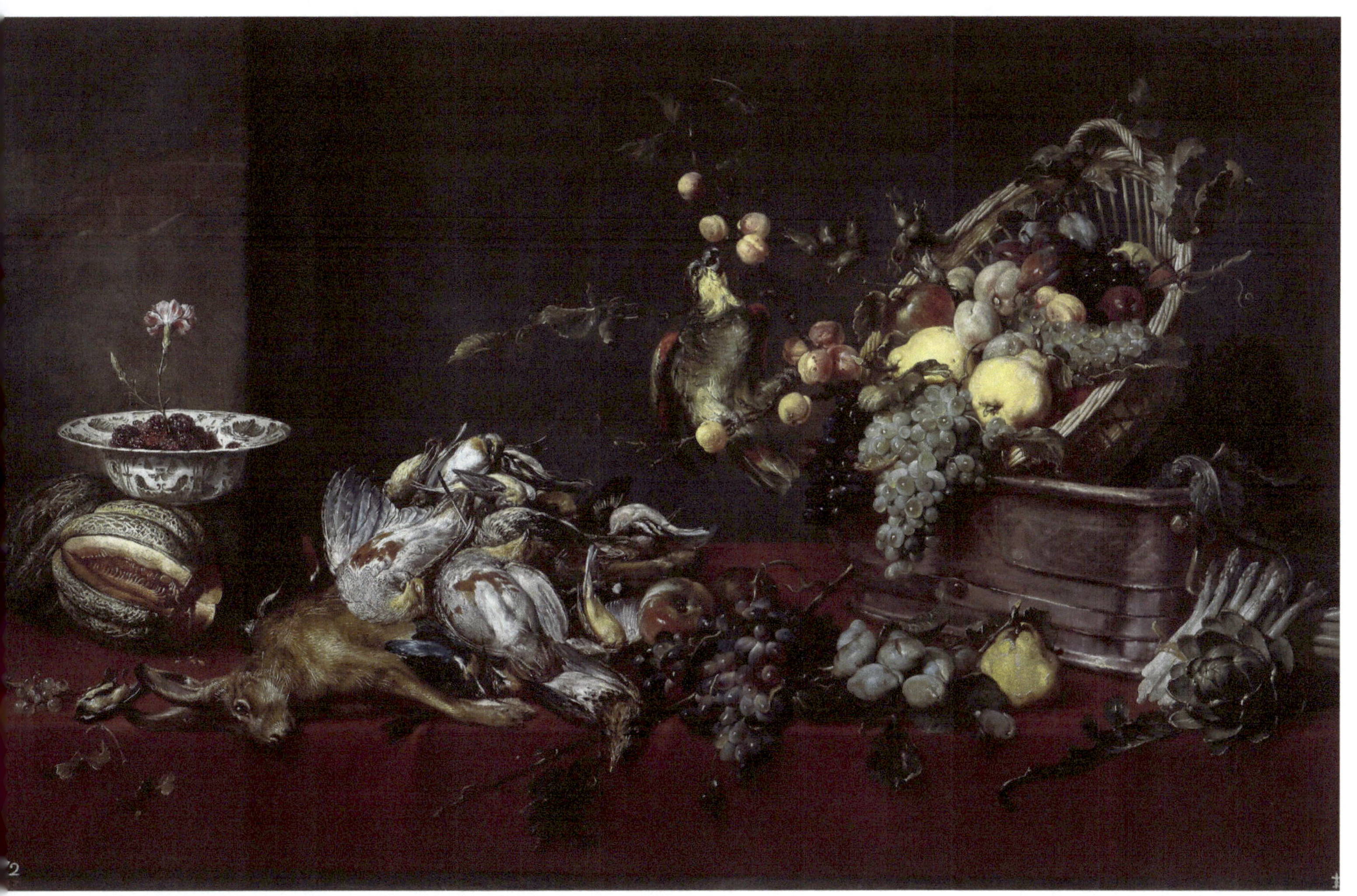

121 x 183 cm

Prado Museum in Madrid

Still life with Game, 1610-20

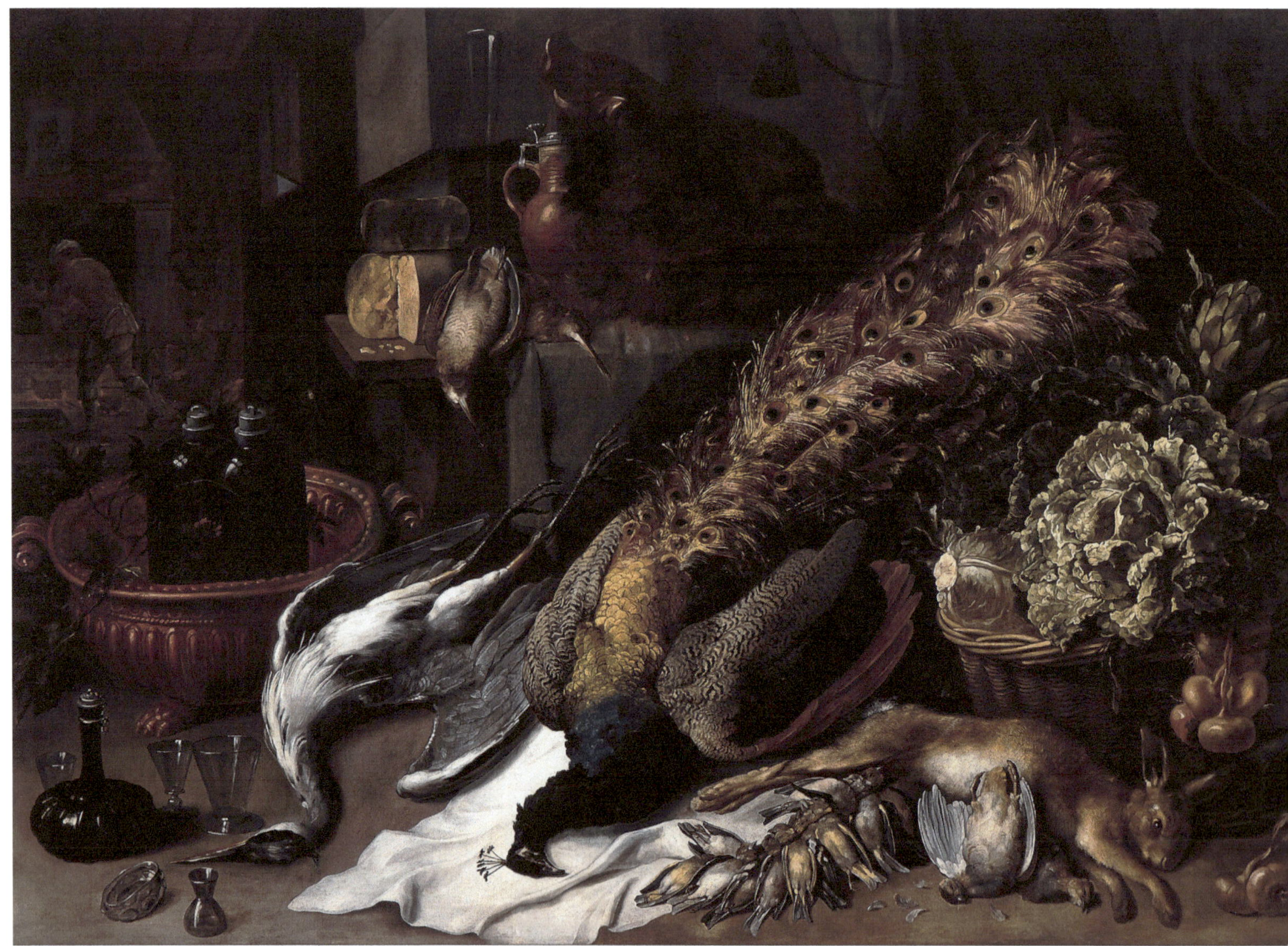

165 x 230 cm

The Banco Santander Foundation in Madrid

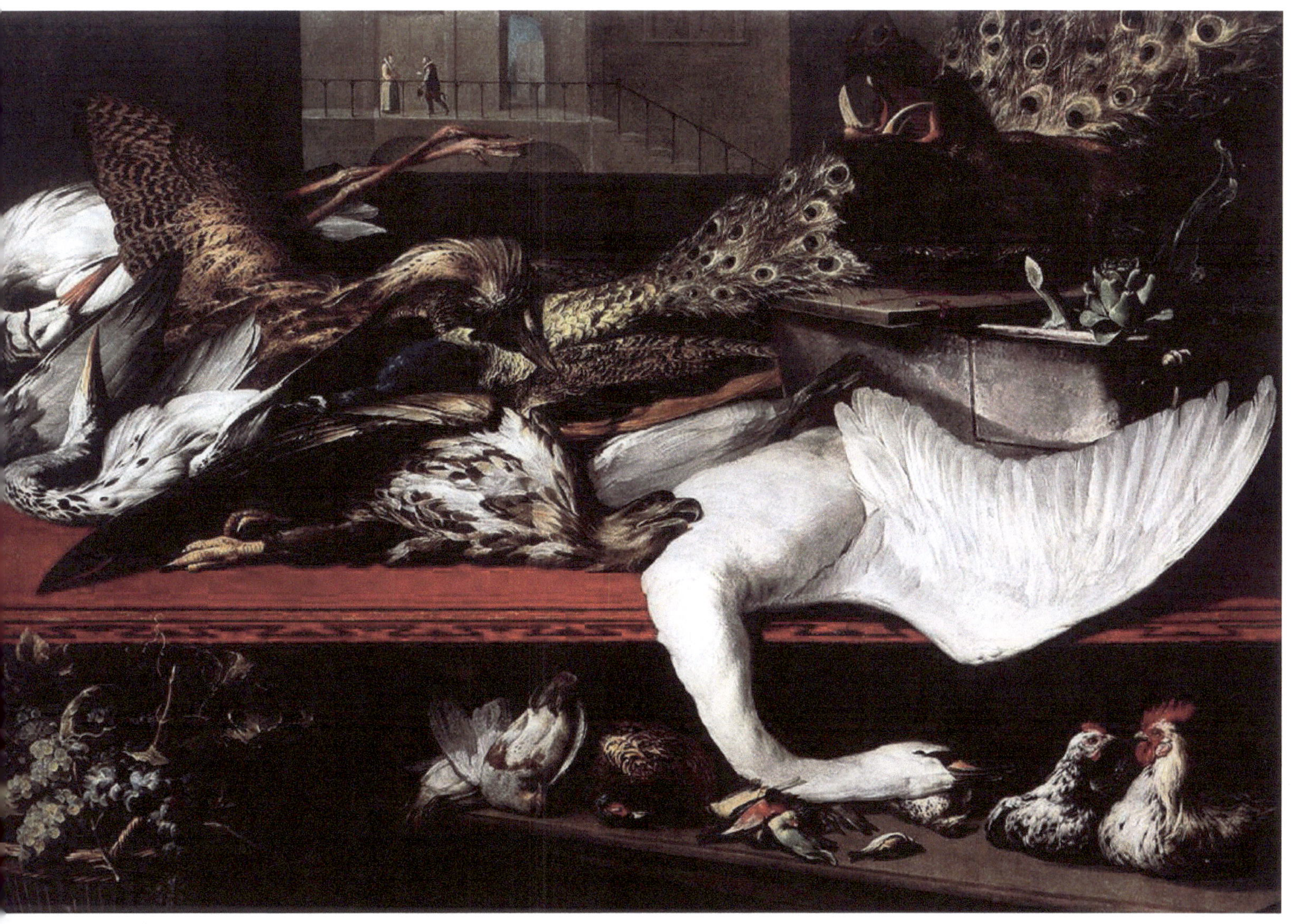

156 x 218 cm

The Wallraf-Richartz Museum in Cologne

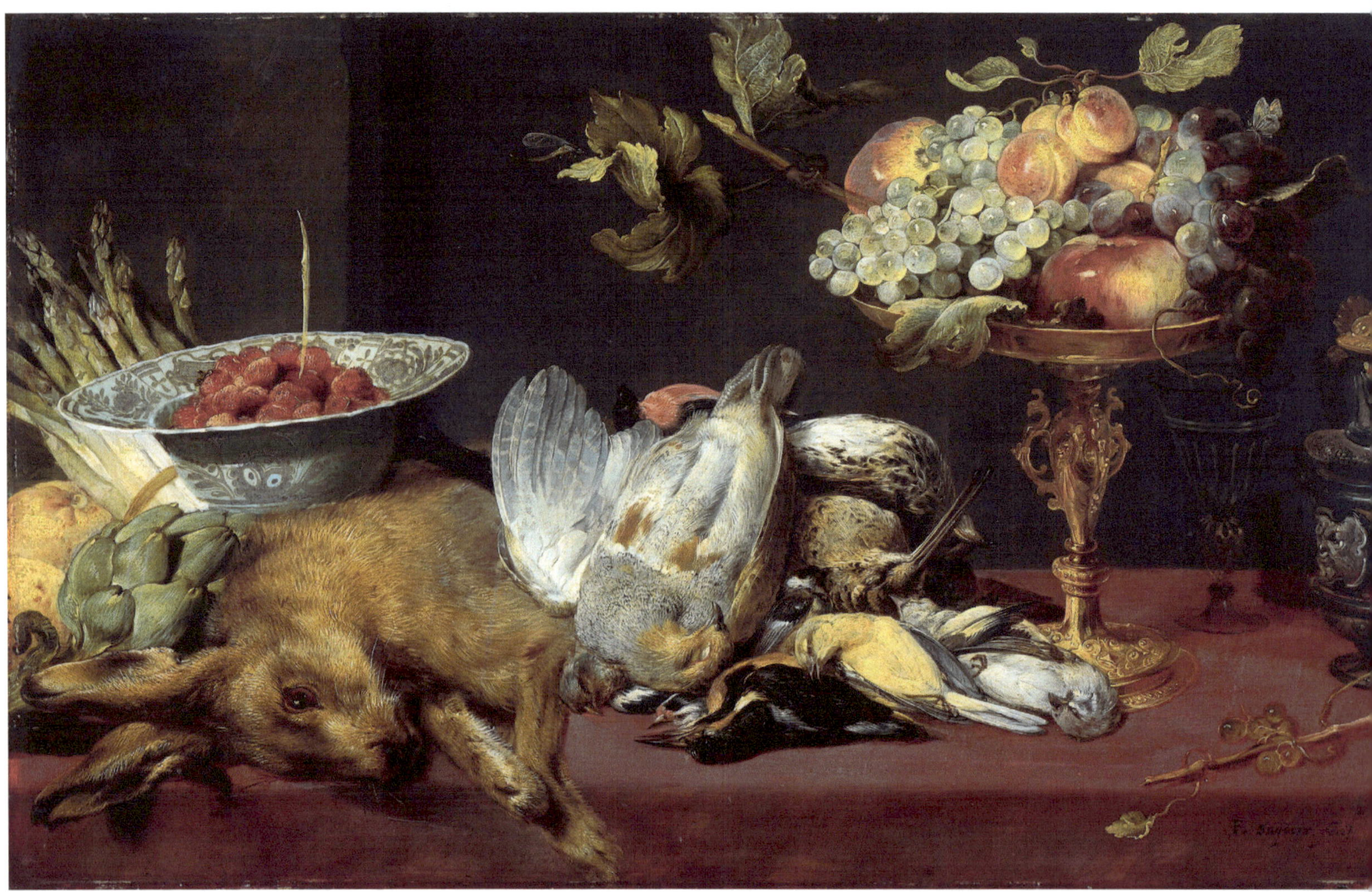

57 x 88 cm

Rijksmuseum Amsterdam

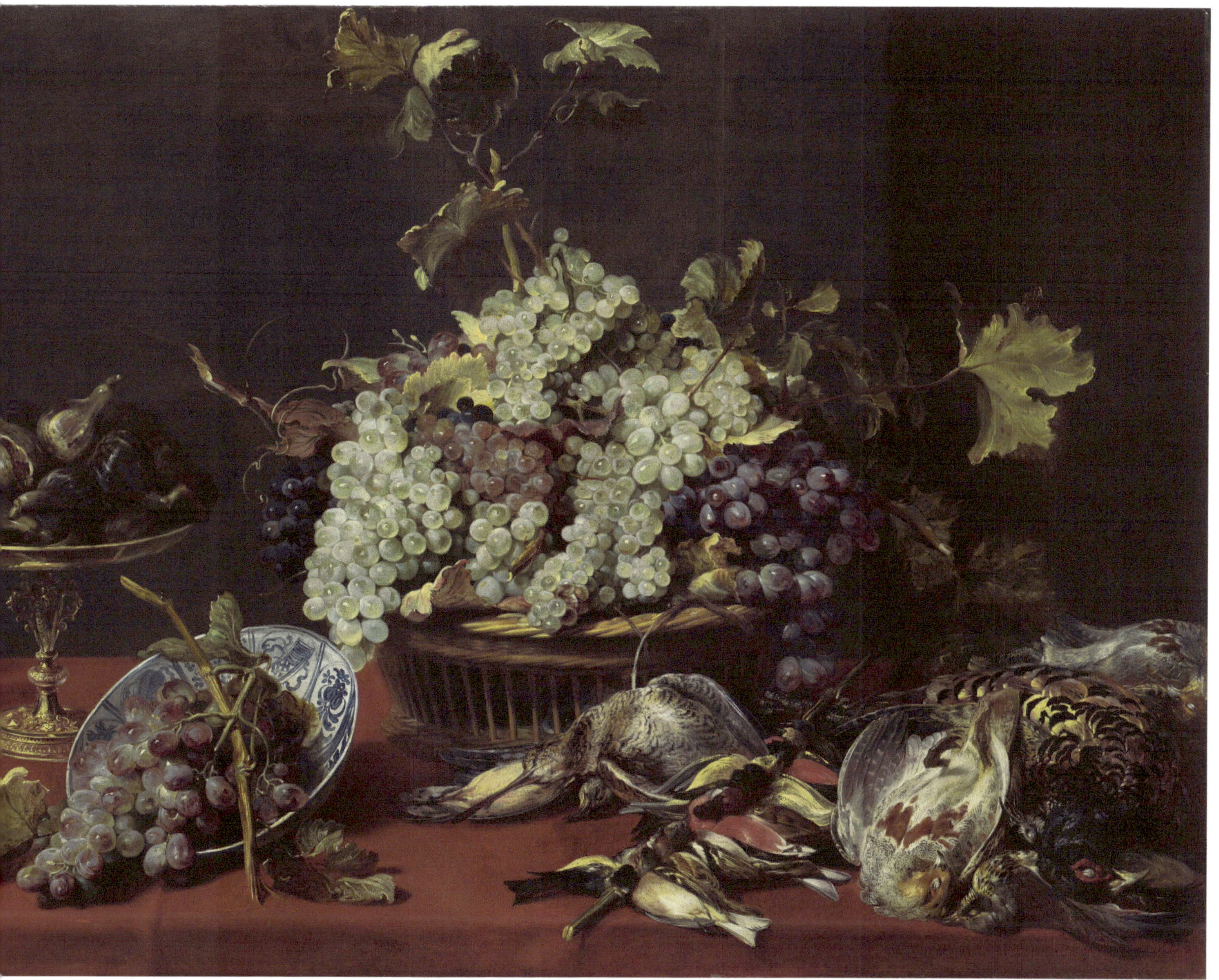

90.2 x 112.1 cm

The National Gallery of Art in Washington, D.C.

Still life with Lobster, c.1615-20

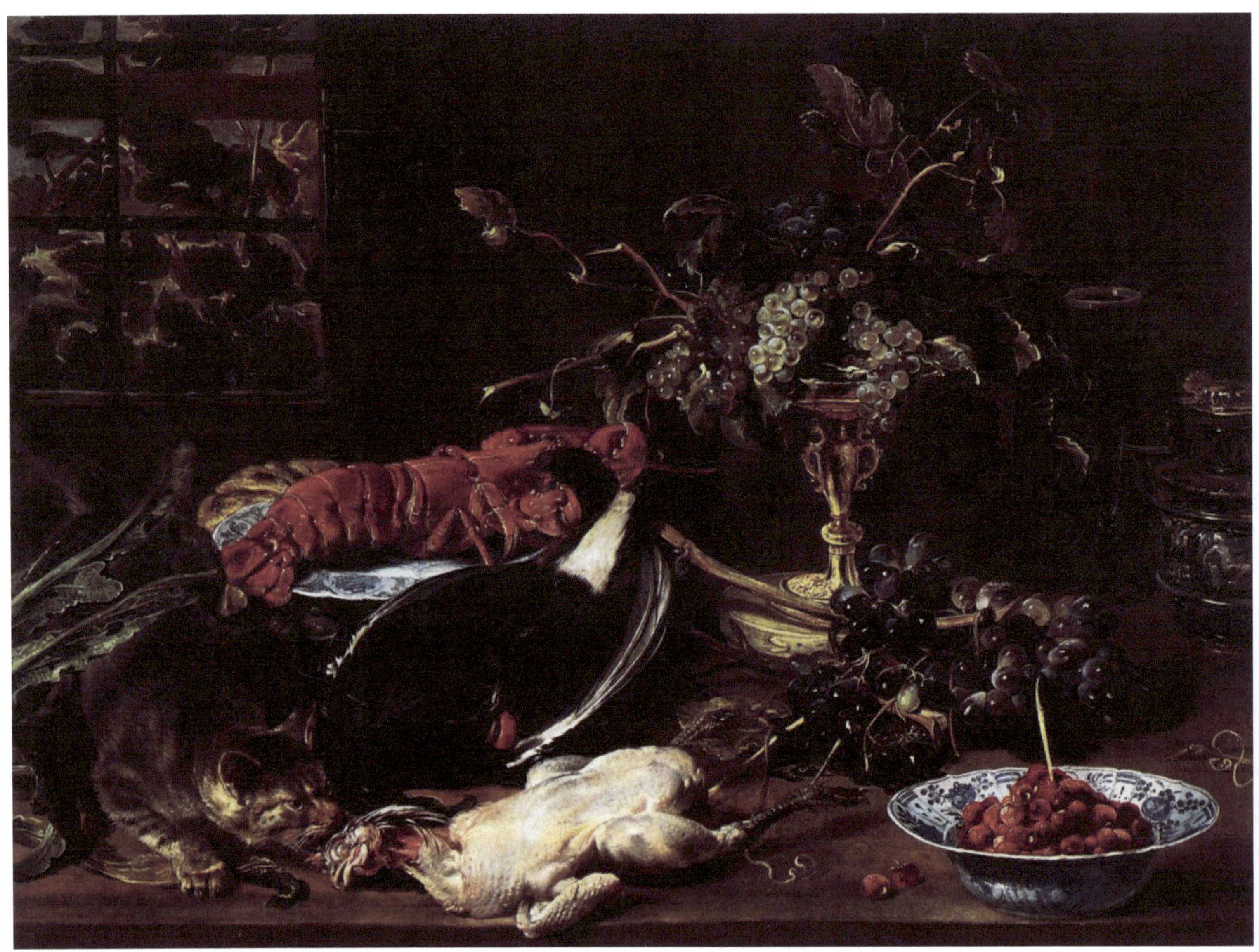

87 x 118 cm

Berlin State Museums

Still life with marmoset, cat and squirrel

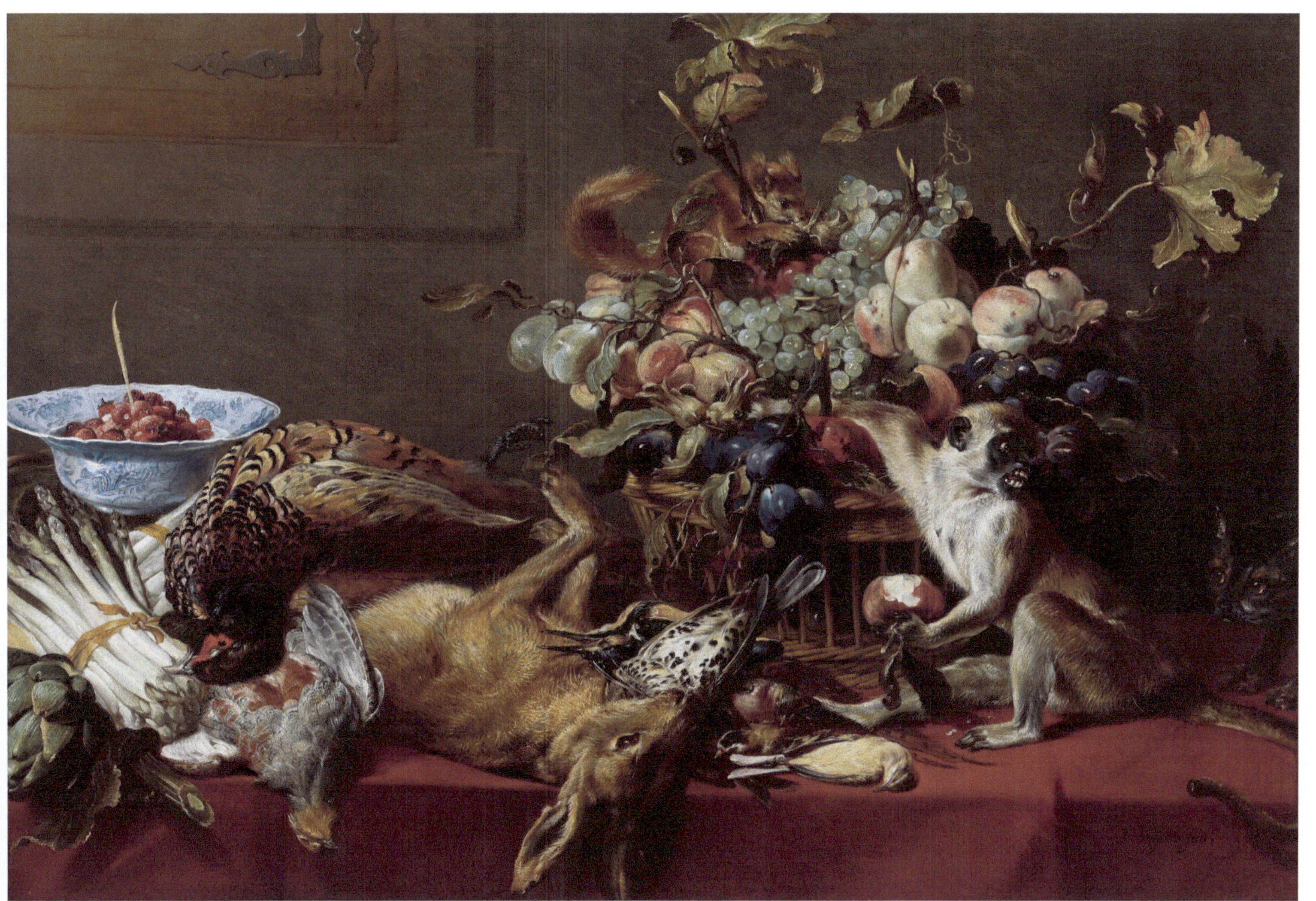

81 x 118 cm

Liechtenstein Museum

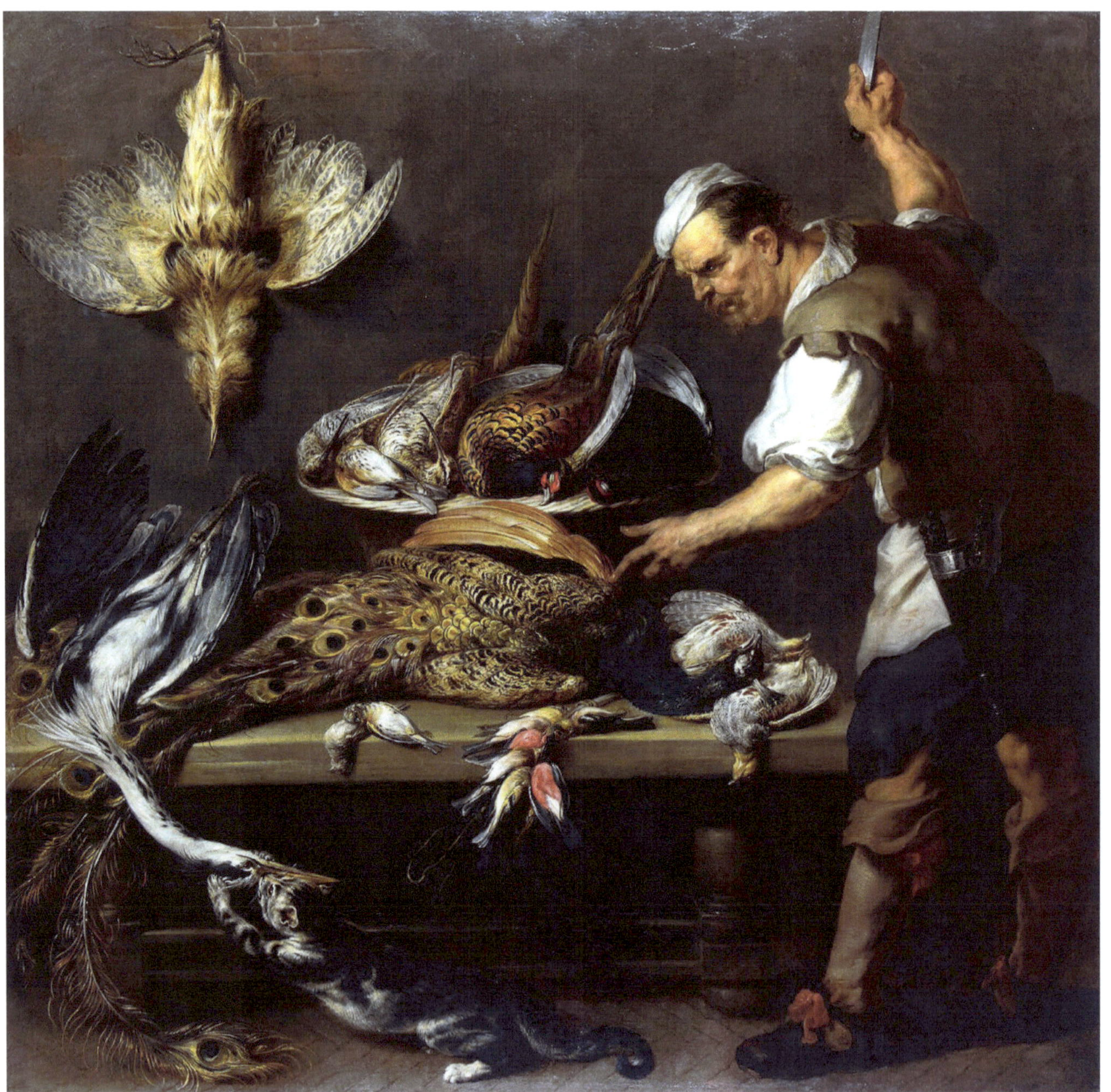

171 x 173 cm

The The State Hermitage Museum in Saint Petersburg

Jan Weenix
c.1641/1649 – 1719

Jan Weenix, born into an artistic household, received his artistic education under his father, Jan Baptist Weenix, who was a painter. He showed exceptional talent in painting landscapes, animals, still lifes, and hunting scenes. Later, he became a pupil of Nicolaes Moeyaert, a landscape painter. Weenix conveyed a sense of luxury to viewers through his realistic depictions and intricate compositions. His paintings gained popularity among the affluent elite, and he received numerous commissions from prominent patrons, including European nobility. Throughout his life, Weenix's style evolved through various approaches. In his later years, he was influenced by Italian art and contemporary artists, transitioning to a more classical and formal style.

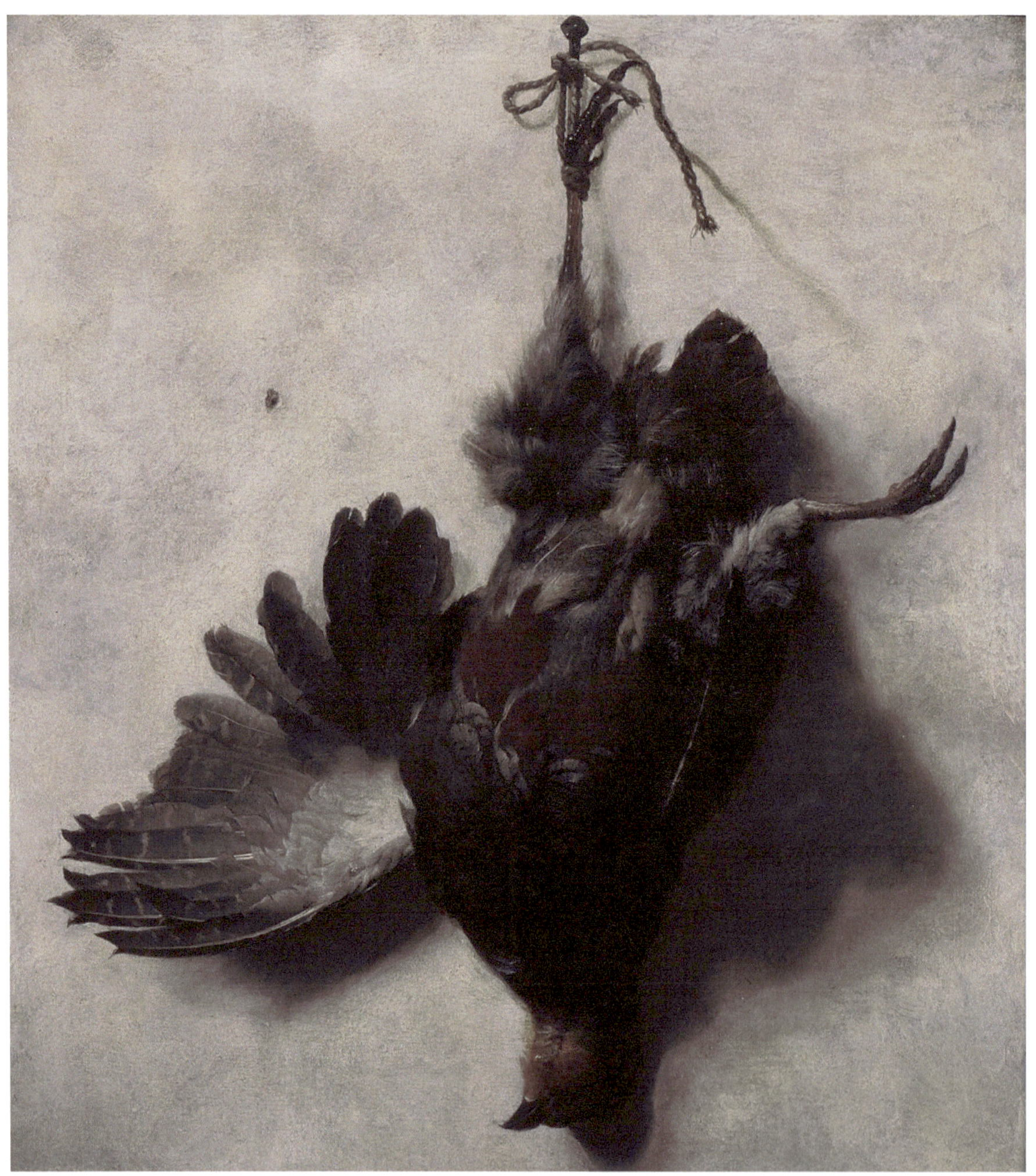

50.6 x 43.5 cm

The Royal Picture Gallery Mauritshuis

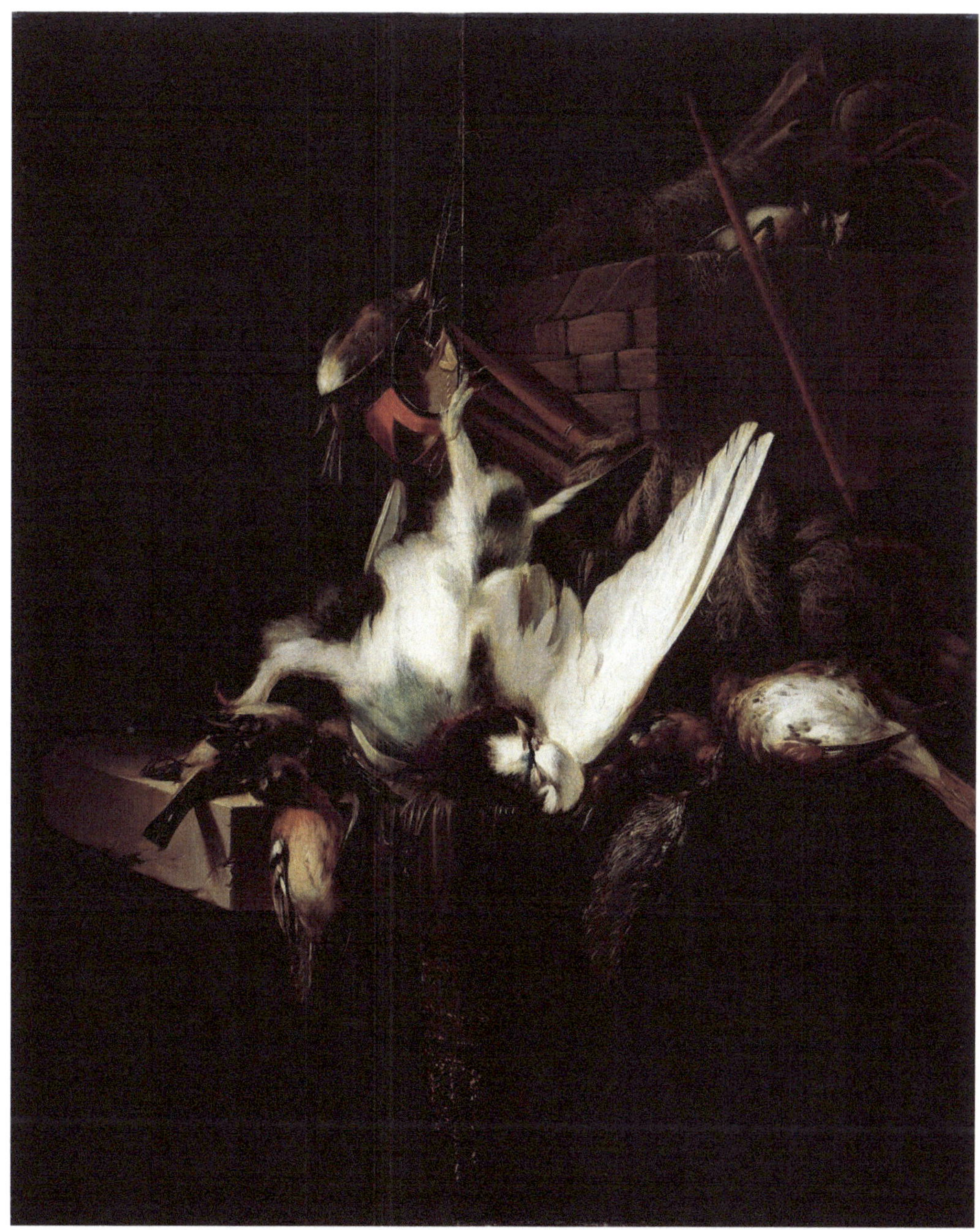

70 x 56 cm

The Liechtenstein Museum in Vienna

Willem Van Aelst
1627 - 1683

    Willem Van Aelst was born on May 16, 1627, in Delft, Netherlands. He was a painter who encompassed both praise for abundance and contemplation of Vanitas, presenting the intricate and thought-provoking compositions characteristic of the still life paintings of the Dutch Golden Age. Van Aelst began his artistic training under his uncle, the prominent still life painter Evert van Aelst. He later became a pupil of his relative Jan Davidsz. de Heem, an influential still life painter of the time. Under the guidance of these two mentors, Van Aelst honed his skills and developed his unique style.

At the age of 16, in 1643, he became a member of the Guild of Saint Luke in Delft, receiving recognition as a professional painter. He later traveled to France, where he worked in the court of Louis XIV for a while as a painter for the French king. After his time in France, Van Aelst returned to the Netherlands and settled in Amsterdam. He achieved considerable fame and success as a still life painter, particularly renowned for his ability to depict extremely realistic textures and intricate details.

His works often featured luxurious objects, exotic flowers, fruits, hunted animals, and other symbolic elements. Through depictions of hunted game, hunting tools, and lush vegetation, he conveyed a sense of abundance. Vivid colors, meticulous details, and carefully arranged elements contributed to the overall opulence and visual splendor. Meanwhile, one can also sense Vanitas aspects introduced. The depiction of animal carcasses not only showcases beauty even in death but also serves as a reminder of the mortality of humans and the transience of life.

The juxtaposition of life and death, abundance and decay, prompts viewers to contemplate the fleeting nature of existence and the ultimate meaninglessness of worldly pursuits. Willem Van Aelst passed away on December 8, 1683, in Amsterdam, at the age of 56. As a prominent still life painter of the Dutch Golden Age, his legacy is preserved in museums and private collections worldwide.

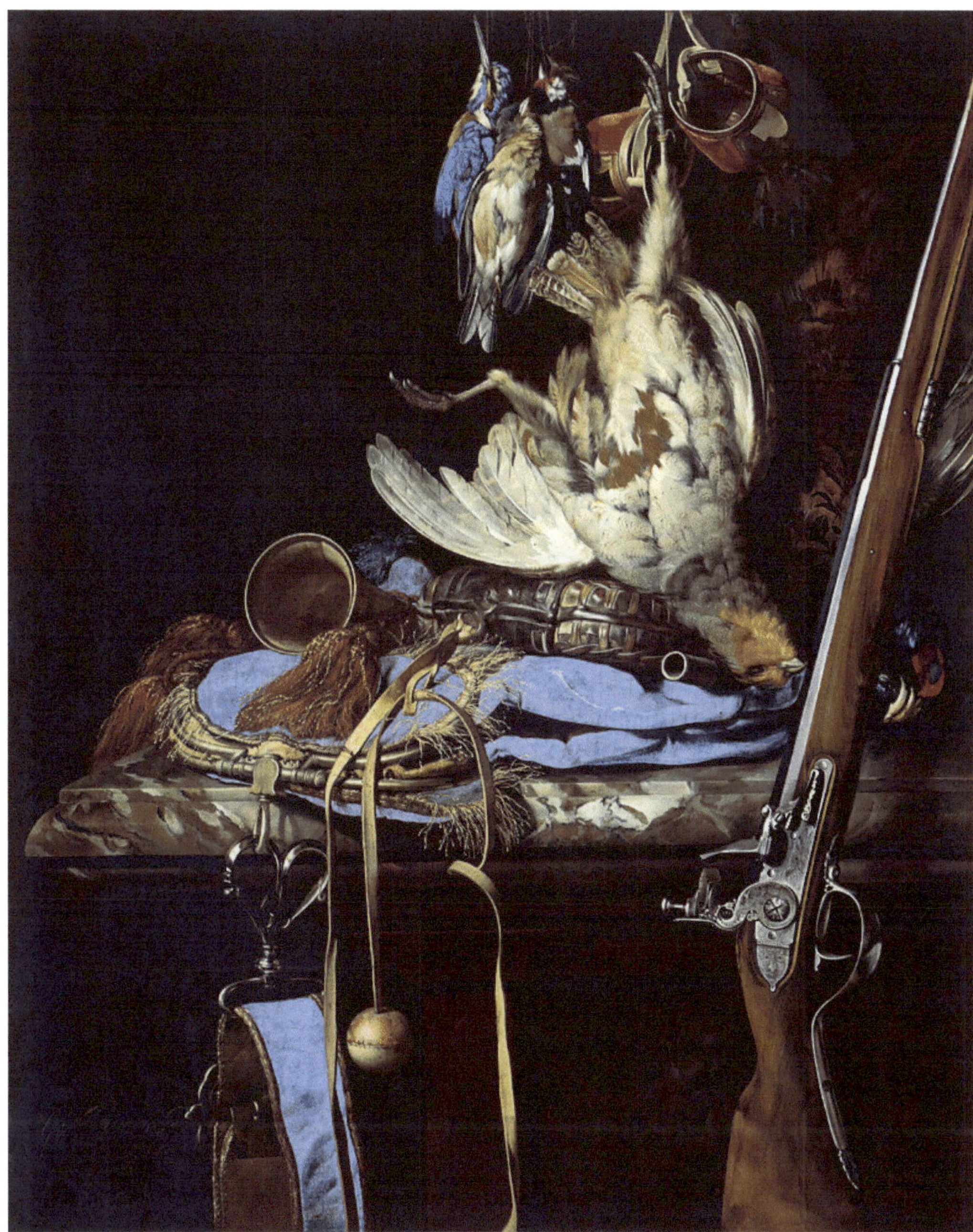

68 x 54 cm

The National Museum in Stockholm

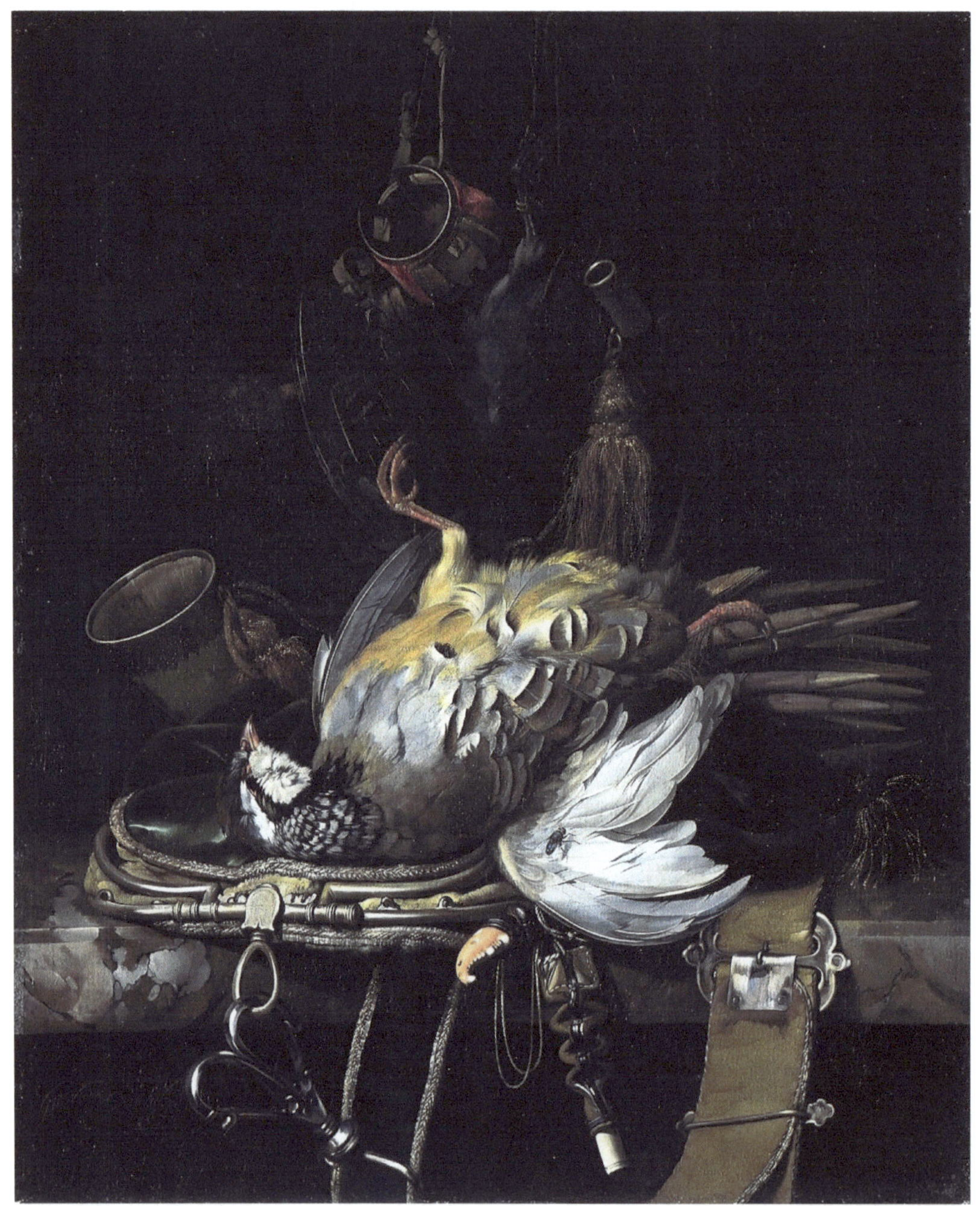

58.8 x 47.8 cm

The Royal Picture Gallery Mauritshuis

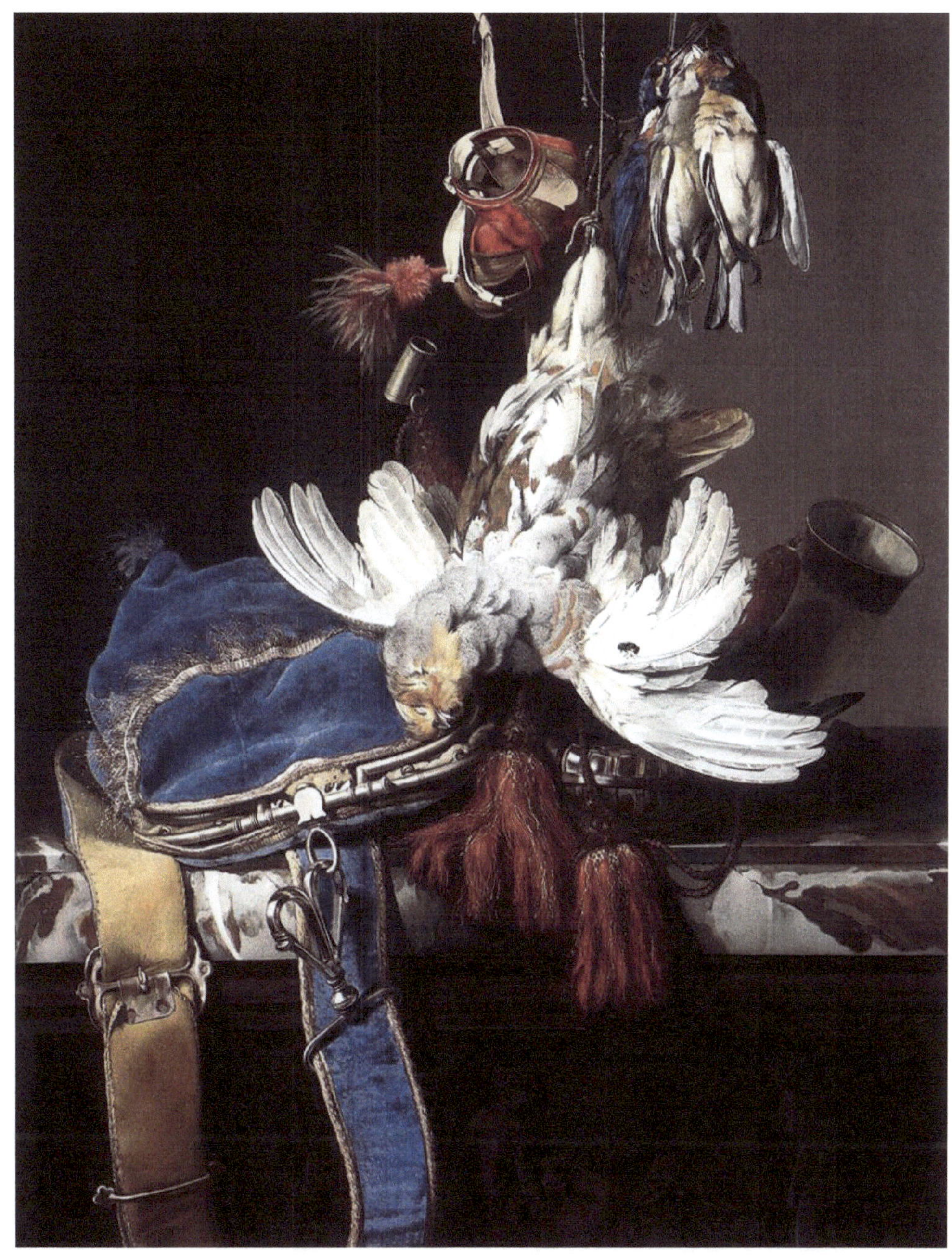

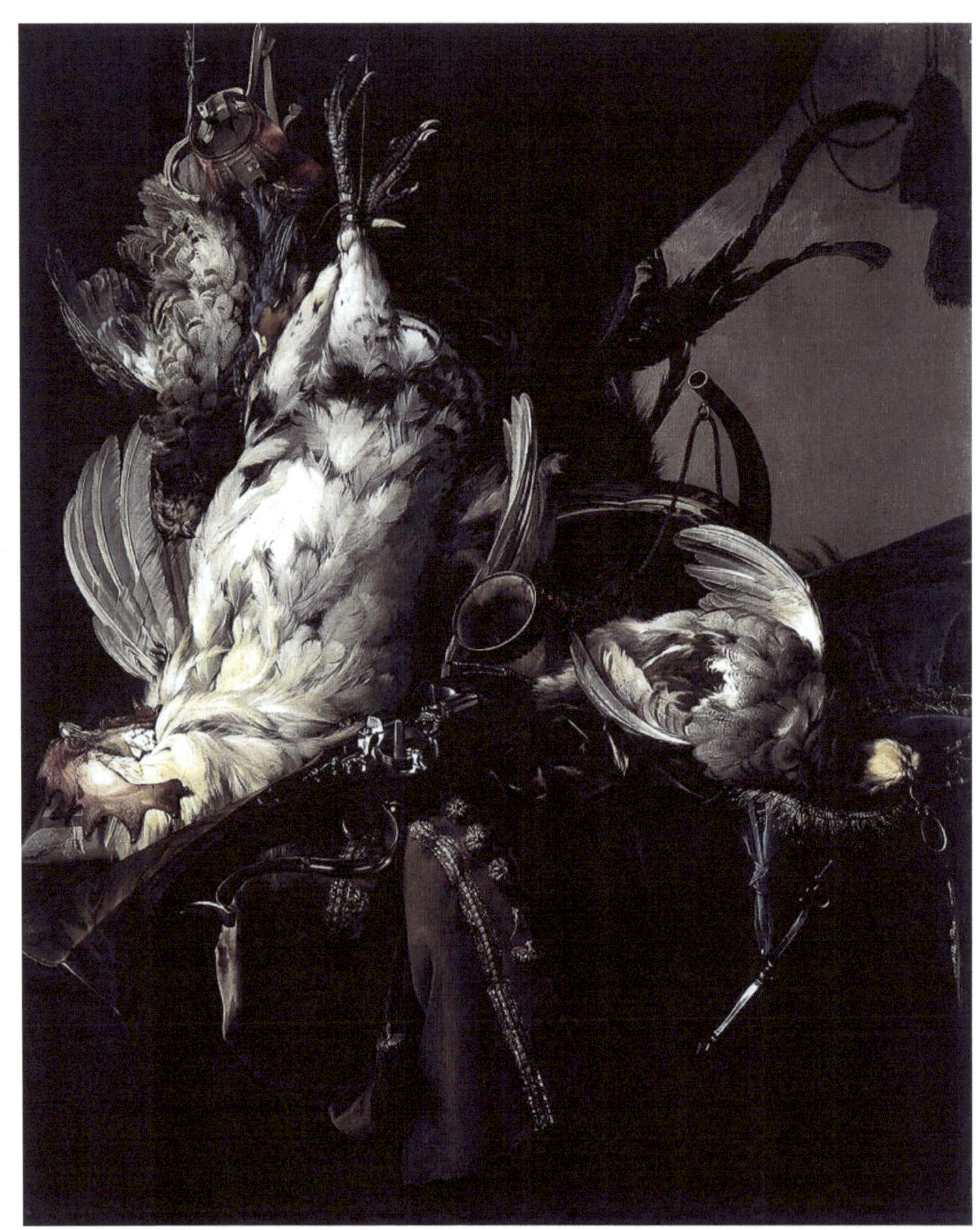

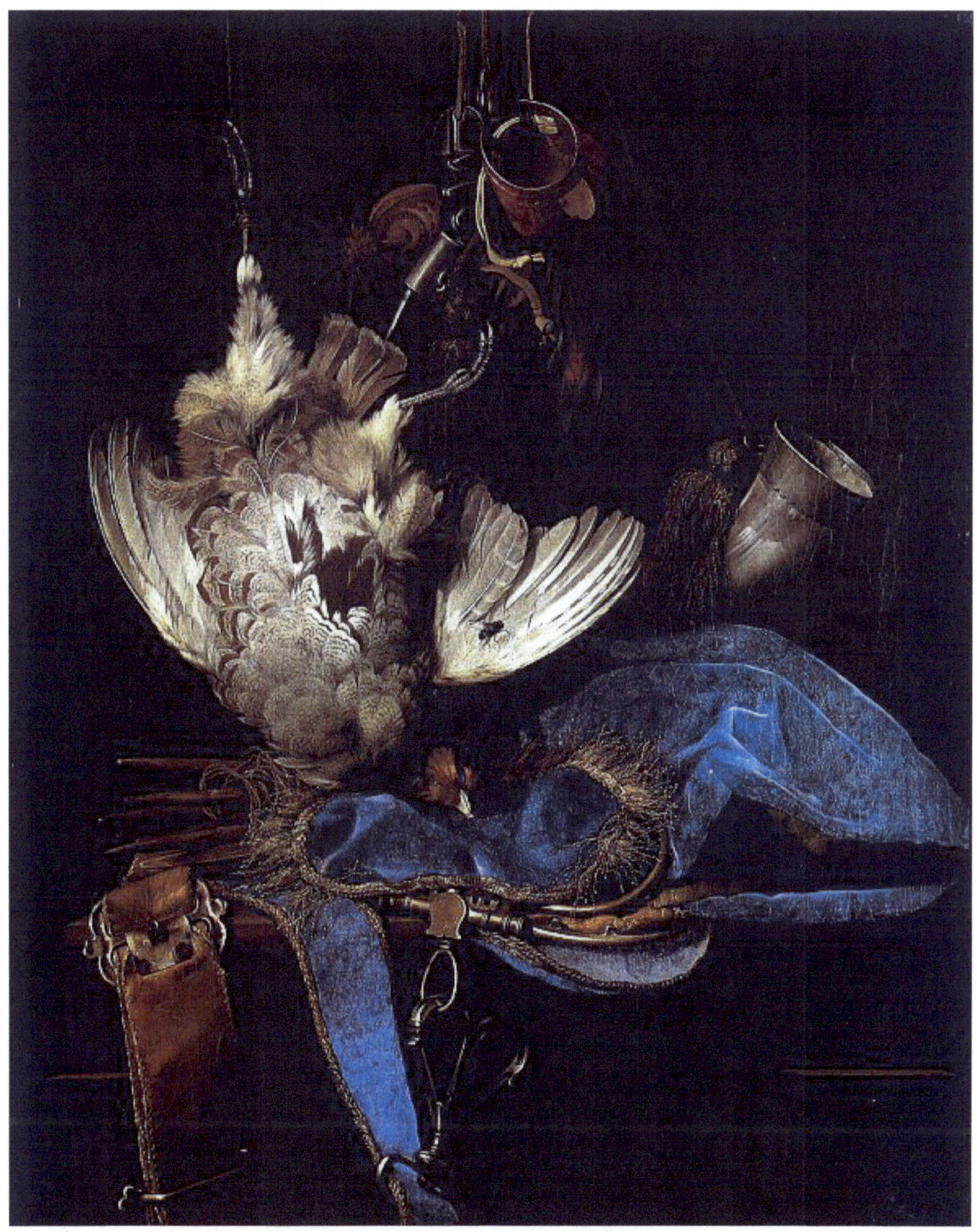

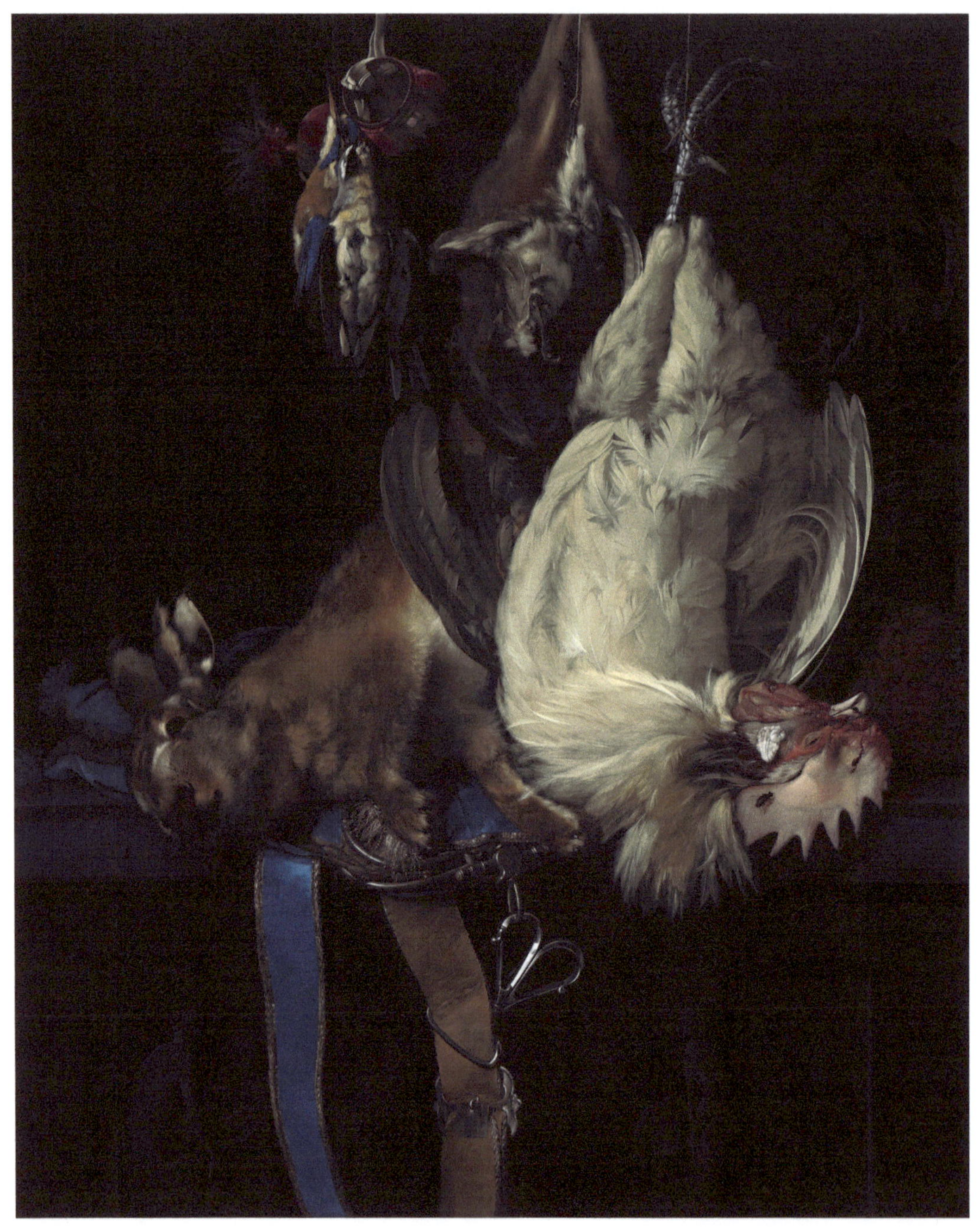

84.7 x 67.3 cm

The National Gallery of Art in Washington, D.C.

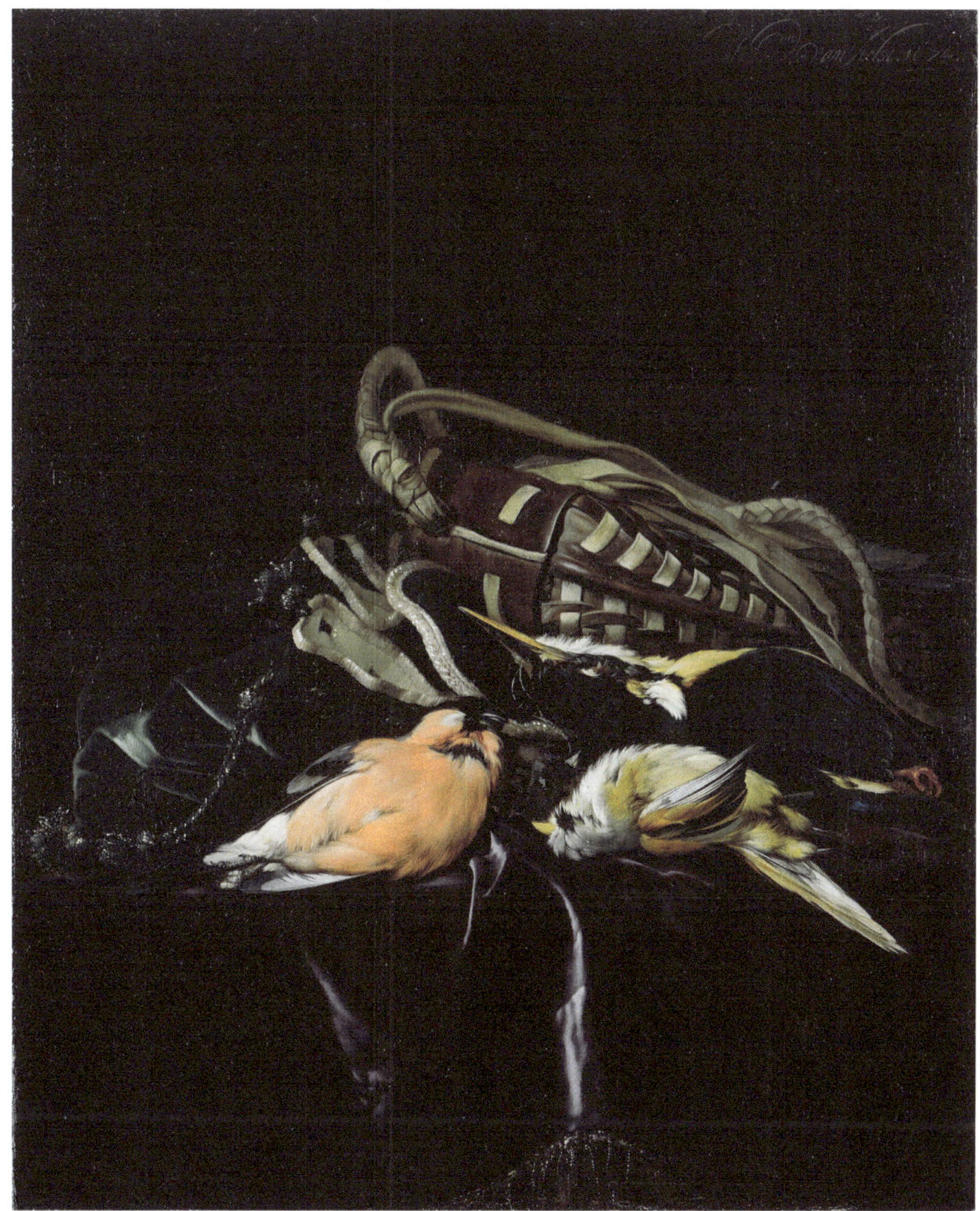

45 x 37 cm

The J. Paul Getty Museum in Los Angeles

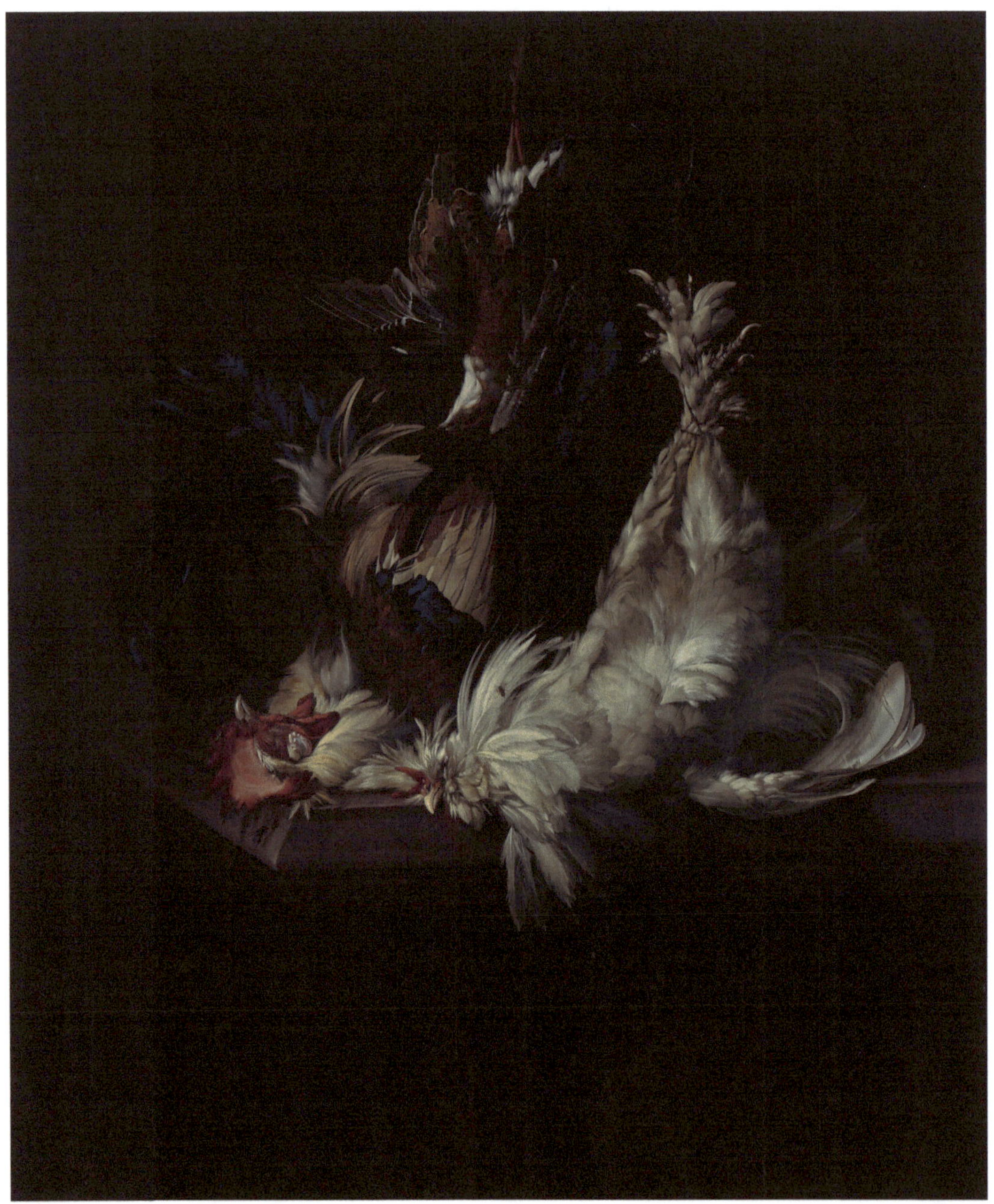

95 x 78.5 cm

Rijksmuseum Amsterdam